READING TOGETHER

Heinemann Educational Books Ltd

LONDON EDINBURGH MELBOURNE TORONTO
SINGAPORE JOHANNESBURG AUCKLAND
IBADAN HONG KONG NAIROBI NEW DELHI

ISBN 0 435 18170 X

Project Director: Frank Whitehead
Research Officer: Kenyon Calthrop
Project Secretary: Jeanne Marshall

Members of the Steering Committee
Douglas Barnes
Gordon Leake
George Long
William Spouge

This investigation into the use of the class reader
was financed by the Calouste Gulbenkian Foundation

Published by
Heinemann Educational Books Ltd
48 Charles Street, London W1X 8AH

Printed in Great Britain
by Butler & Tanner Ltd, Frome and London

READING TOGETHER

An investigation into the
use of the class reader

KENYON CALTHROP

Department of Education
The Trent Polytechnic

Published for the
National Association for the
Teaching of English
by Heinemann Educational Books Ltd

CONTENTS

PREFACE

I am deeply grateful to a great many people who made this Project possible and without whom nothing could have been achieved.

I would like to thank the Gulbenkian Foundation for their willingness to finance it and the Sheffield Education Committee for their generous provision of office space and equipment.

I would like to thank the Principal and Governing Body of the City of Leicester College of Education for granting me a year's leave of absence in order to undertake the Project, and my colleagues in the English Department at that College for putting up with a great deal while this Report was nearing completion.

I would like to thank the members of my steering committee for their interest, suggestions and concern, and an ex-student of mine, Miss Sylvia Deveson, for invaluable assistance in evaluating and collating much raw material.

I would like to thank Mr George Cardew of the University of Sheffield for the calculations involved in attempting to assess some children's reactions to some of the books, and Mr Peter Brown of the Mathematics Department at Leicester College of Education for checking those calculations.

I would like to thank the Project Secretary, Mrs Jeanne Marshall, who loyally adapted herself to whatever the Project demanded, with an unselfish conscientiousness.

I would like very particularly to thank the Project Director, Frank Whitehead, for his experienced wisdom, understanding and sympathetic advice.

Lastly, I would like to thank many members of the teaching profession; the Headmaster and Staff of Philadelphia County Primary School, Sheffield, for much kindness and welcoming hospitality; the many English teachers who sweated over my original questionnaire and who gave unstintingly of their time; and the Heads and English Departments of the schools who willingly allowed me to visit them and who put up with much inconvenience and interrogation.

This is their Report as much as it is mine, although I alone am responsible for the faults it contains.

KENYON CALTHROP

INTRODUCTION

In 1966 the Calouste Gulbenkian Foundation very generously awarded a grant to the National Association for the Teaching of English to make possible a Curriculum Project concerned with Literature (Prose Books) in English Teaching between the ages of eleven and sixteen. The need for such a project had been justified to the Gulbenkian Foundation in the following terms:

Informed opinion at the present time is agreed about the centrality of literature (broadly conceived) in the teaching of English, and stress has rightly been laid, in many quarters, on the importance for children's personal and linguistic development of the experience they obtain from reading. Even at the utilitarian level of effective command of language there is powerful support for the belief that much of the time now spent in the classroom on 'English exercises' and work from course books would be better spent in the reading of 'real books'. Many teachers, however, remain uncertain about the precise forms which the teaching of literature should take, and urgently need guidance as to choice of material for particular types and levels of pupil and as to the best methods of handling this material. At the same time the best teachers in our secondary schools have accumulated a wealth of experience of such work which remains too little diffused.

The Curriculum Project proposed was in essence a 'user-survey' concerned with the best current practice making use in schools of prose books—novels, short-story volumes, biographies, etc. In September 1967 Kenyon Calthrop took up the post of Research Officer to the Project, having been seconded for one year to devote himself to the work full-time. The first step was to draw up and circulate a questionnaire which would gather from secondary school teachers reports about work carried out with particular prose books which they had found outstandingly successful with more than one class of a given type and age level. The questionnaire also gave space for additional information about the approach and methods of handling adopted by the teacher, and the extremely interesting material included under this heading has been drawn on extensively in the present Report. More than six hundred questionnaires were returned by teachers in different parts of the country, and the readiness of teachers to share with others the successes they had enjoyed with their own pupils has provided the basis from which Mr Calthrop has been able to paint a most illuminating picture of current practice in this area of English teaching in secondary schools. During the first half of 1968 Mr Calthrop visited a number of the classes reported upon in order to study the pupils' reactions and attitudes at first hand. This visiting was intended in part as a check upon the validity of the Teacher-Reports, and in general the impression given above all was that the teachers concerned had indeed a very shrewd and realistic picture of what was going on in their classrooms and how their pupils felt about it. In addition, the visits did provide some vivid first-hand additional detail which Mr Calthrop has been able to incorporate in places into his final report.

I have no doubt that the resulting volume does provide a great deal of material that will be extremely helpful to teachers seeking to improve and diversify their classroom practice. The practising teacher is as a rule very much confined to his own classroom and has little opportunity to visit other teachers actually at work. For his sense of the ways in which colleagues in other classrooms confront and overcome problems parallel to his own he must rely largely on reporting at second hand. Here are a number of such reports, carefully sifted, and arranged so as to give as much practical help and suggestion as possible. The book provides, in fact, a window into other classrooms, and the view through that window seems to me encouraging and even inspiring.

FRANK WHITEHEAD

Chapter One

THE CLASS READER

THE HISTORICAL BACKGROUND

The investigations of A. J. Jenkinson thirty years ago[1] showed that much of the devotion and skill of the English teachers of the day was ineffective, because the class texts in use at that time failed to take into account the real needs of developing adolescents. Further, the adult tastes imposed on the children resulted in many children enduring books 'which for the most part they have neither understood nor enjoyed'.

What Jenkinson describes as the 'grim inexorability' of most middle school English courses is borne out by his tabulated lists of books in use in schools. Twelve-year-olds in the then senior schools were ploughing through extracts from *The Cloister and the Hearth* or *Gallant Deeds*. At thirteen (their last year in school), *Selected Essays (Addison to Lynd)* was regarded as suitable fare, together with *Gateways to Bookland*.

The children in the junior forms of secondary schools read from a list of books of a kind which is probably still in use in some grammar schools and which certainly differs very little from the experiences of some of my College of Education students some ten years ago. From fourteen onwards the choice (as now) tended to be prescribed by the external examiners. Their choice (of prose works) consisted of plenty of models for 'good writing'. The de Coverley Papers, Peacock's, Lamb's, and Goldsmith's Essays feature prominently in Jenkinson's list, which concludes for good measure with *Three Centuries of English Essays*. For the less fanciful there were

[1] A. J. Jenkinson, *What Do Boys and Girls Read?*, Methuen, 1940.

such titles as *Eyewitness Accounts of Scenes of Action* or *Drake's World Encompassed*.

Conversations with those of my colleagues who were at school themselves in the twenties and thirties confirm that the kind of list which Jenkinson tabulated stretches back, almost unaltered, at least to the twenties. However, as a result of Jenkinson's work, English teachers in the 1940s began to take more account of the real needs, natural interests and private reading habits of their pupils. Moreover the impact of Jenkinson's findings began to show itself in the lists of the more enterprising publishers, who made available in attractively produced school editions an increasingly wide range of modern copyright material. (A good example of the new trend was the appearance in 1950 of Heinemann's *New Windmill Series* under the editorship of Ian Serraillier.)

Today it is clear that in terms of choice of material the schools have never been better served. The standard classics are available in a bewildering variety of editions and the number of modern titles from which to choose is still increasing steadily.

Parallel with this diversification of publishers' lists, there has been a continual expansion and improvement in public library services; and the revolution in paperback publishing has also reached schools directly in such schemes as Scholastic Publications' Paperback Readers Club for Schools. Thus as far as the availability of material is concerned, the encouragement of all kinds of reading in schools is easier than it has ever been.

It is perhaps not surprising therefore that the reports from the teachers who took part in our Survey reflect this variety. The total number of titles which teachers reported as having used successfully was 221, yet there were only 28 titles where five or more teachers reported on the same book.

A SHARED EXPERIENCE

All the teachers I interviewed felt that the shared experience of reading a common book was something of great value to themselves and to their classes. They regarded it as something quite different from the pleasure to be gained from individual reading and took the view that the feeling of sharing something worth while, the common sense of enjoyment, and the resulting sense of community was a deeply educative process.[1] It is perhaps significant that these teachers see this as very much a reciprocal process, i.e. an atmosphere in which the children respond to the teacher and the teacher responds to the class.

A few teachers went so far as to suggest that this process was something akin to the experience of a theatre audience, and that it was this which gave the reading of a book together an intangible quality which was very different from an individual reading. The whole process involved a performance by the teacher, a collective, but enjoyed and shared, response from the audience, together with a fair amount of audience participation. As one very successful grammar school teacher put it, somewhat flippantly perhaps, 'Any successful English teaching involves an element of mountebankery. I do enjoy the mountebankery bit myself and I can dignify it as a "shared experience".'

In introducing children to literature, some teachers felt that the child often needed a shared literary experience. Further, if the book in question related to life, the teacher was also extending the child's shared experience of life and the children could share their responses to the very relevant experience which the book provided. One teacher summed it up thus: 'The process of common response to a common book is deeply educative, not by brainwashing, but by the initiative coming from them [i.e. the children]. They couldn't have the same experience without a common book.'

Another very successful and committed teacher, in charge of the C Stream children in a large mixed urban secondary modern school, felt this very strongly, thinking particularly of the kind of child he was directly concerned with.

A lot of the secondary modern child's difficulties come through isolation. They're timid in sampling new words, they

[1] One Head of Department in a secondary modern school I visited, felt that this process of drawing in the children together was of such value that it helped in the discipline in the school, throughout the notoriously difficult third year.

tend to go round in a rut. In a world of competition they're going to fail—a lot of them think they're failures anyway. It is very important that they have co-operative ventures—shared experiences. It is normal for an infant teacher to read her children a story, this is a shared experience which they enjoy. In many families reading can be a shared experience, older children read to younger—everyone stops and listens. With a class, such as the one you saw this morning—a shared experience, but more than this, we all have the book for points of reference. A shared experience where they have a copy [of the book] makes them happier, even where they don't fully understand it. Think of the young child in a family who can't read, holding his book for the reader.

READING ALOUD

The Teacher Reading
Despite the analogy drawn by the teacher above, it is doubtful whether enough children, at whatever age, experience much family reading. 'Children love a story and will willingly listen to a good one—possibly this is something they don't get from their parents'; this from a teacher of younger grammar school children in a very deprived area. Other teachers I spoke to (of whatever age!) remembered very clearly the intensity with which they listened to the teacher reading during their own primary school days.

Clearly this affectionate retrospection has something to do with the shared experience I have already referred to, but there are other considerations. Some teachers held that the sound of the written words was important. The sound of literature should be in the ears as well as in the mind, as this has a great deal to do with the quality of understanding. Put more simply, this gives the book an extra dimension which children reading to themselves are unable to find. A skilled reader can bring out the qualities of a book in a way which the children are unable to do for themselves—this reading need not necessarily come from the teacher, it could be on tape, and the number of gramophone records suitable for this purpose is slowly increasing (e.g. Longmans Series of recordings of short stories—some read by the authors themselves). A good reading

4

can also enable the children to experience literature which would otherwise be beyond their understanding. One comprehensive school teacher mentioned for example the Muriel Spark short story *You Should Have Seen the Mess*, the irony of which would be appreciated fairly readily by the middle-class sophisticated child, but which needed a 'performed' reading to be understood at all by his pupils.

There are times when, for one particular purpose or another, perhaps in using a short story or an extract from a longer book, the teacher will have the only copy. However, at other times, and probably more frequently, the children ought to have their own copies in front of them. The less able the child, the more important this is, since the linking of the heard reading with the printed word helps them with their own inner reading.

There are implications here for teacher training. 'It is amazing when Miss X reads, but when Miss Y reads, it just comes out like a string of words.' Some of the teachers I spoke to had the courage to admit that their own 'public' reading was not as effective as they would have liked it to have been; several senior and highly experienced English teachers felt that most teachers' reading was simply not good enough.

The Children Reading
One of the assumptions of those opposed to the class reader is that its use implies a dreary reading round the class which quickly kills any real interest in the story, while the qualities of the book are submerged by the common mechanical struggle with the words on the page.

Some of the teachers of more intelligent children felt that it was particularly important to this kind of child to be able to read aloud well. They did not feel that, with intelligent children, there were any real obstacles to the enjoyment of the book by the rest of the class. One teacher in a girls' grammar school used the opportunity given her by the girls' reading aloud to assess very carefully their reactions to the book. At the same time these teachers felt that it was important to do a good deal of reading themselves.

However, the children capable of this are very much in a

minority. In the past we have certainly underestimated what we are demanding of children in asking them to read aloud 'off the cuff', and most children will never be able to read aloud spontaneously well enough to avoid doing an injustice to the writer and boring their fellows. The mistake we have made in the past is in expecting the children to do this unprepared. Any reading we expect of them must be prepared thoroughly and presented as something in the nature of a performance, so that the mechanical difficulties are rehearsed and overcome before the rest of the class are involved.

READING IN DEPTH

One of the most remarkable and forthright teachers I met regarded the class reader as 'the rock of English teaching'. She felt very strongly that any book read in common could be explored much more deeply with the children and that it was part of the English teacher's function to teach the children to read in depth as well as with enthusiasm. (This was in a secondary modern school and was a philosophy applied equally to all streams.) She was not the only teacher to take the view that while one was naturally concerned with reading for enjoyment one was also teaching a skill, and that children needed to be taught to look for deeper significance and, therefore, gain a deeper satisfaction, which was far more fundamental than any superficial enjoyment.

Again this is only possible with a common text and, of course, it works at many different levels. There are the children for whom the reading of any full-length novel at all represents a very considerable achievement. A child of this kind is helped tremendously by being in a class of mixed reading ability and by the discussion and other kinds of activity which accompany the reading of the book.

At another level, a grammar school G.C.E. 'O' level Literature class, who had clearly been very well taught and prepared for the examination incidentally, said that they had enjoyed their detailed study of *Lord of the Flies* as it had given them a technique to enrich their whole future way of reading.

DISCUSSION

All the teachers I interviewed regarded the discussion which accompanied the reading of the book as an important and integral part of the experience of it. They thought this kind of discussion valuable because it was founded upon a common base of information and ideas. The reticent child is far more likely to bring forward his ideas when the whole class is engaged in a common discussion; and the brighter members of the class and those who are particularly enjoying the book give something (far more effectively than the teacher can) to those who are struggling. This process of cross-fertilization feeds back both into the child's individual reading and into his writing. To ignore the benefits of this kind of discussion is to remove the only advantage of being in a class. A secondary modern teacher summed it up like this.

A class reader gets them to put forward their own views about the book in a convincing manner, listening to views other children have put forward, so that they can defend their own or admit the relevance of someone else's. Otherwise they become very wrapped up in their own individual interpretation and perhaps miss other views that are very relevant. Some children have not yet [i.e. first two years in the secondary modern school] reached the stage where they can become as completely involved and interested when reading on their own—they wouldn't enjoy it in the same way, because they don't get actual views given to or taken from them.

FOCAL POINT FOR OTHER ACTIVITIES

Many progressive teachers of English have now abandoned the course book altogether and endeavour to make the whole of their English teaching literature or activity based. This demands a great deal more of the teacher than the traditional course-book approach, which at least provided the imaginative and unimaginative teacher alike with a clear-cut and stable framework within which to operate. One of the dangers in our more enlightened approach is that we haven't always considered carefully enough how we are going to replace the framework which the traditional course book, however in-adequately, provided. It is dangerously easy to follow one ambitious project with another, to dream up an ingenious and fruitful scheme of thematic work and then yet another, without stopping to ask ourselves what it will all add up to at the end.

I am convinced by the teachers I interviewed that part of the answer to this is sometimes to regard the class reader (as pre-viously we regarded the course book) as the springboard and focal point of all kinds of related activities. (I am not sug-gesting that it is the only possible springboard, nor am I deprecating thematic work or project work based on other resources.)

This is something the individual reader cannot do. As a preparatory schoolmaster put it to me, 'I feel this is a sort of compromise between the old textbook, which nobody now really thinks very good, and just having nothing at all, where one is apt to lose one's way. I think that with a book like this [*Moonfleet* by J. Meade Falkner] you have a basis for teaching.'

Further, the use of the class reader in this way enables the teacher to abolish the false distinctions between language and literature and find a ready-made unity in all his English teach-ing. 'You use a book like *The History of Mr Polly* for quite a lot of language teaching as well as literature. I don't really dis-tinguish between them—we burnt the grammar books years ago. All that the syllabus consists of is reading, writing and speaking, as it comes out. The language teaching is literature based and we don't use any course books at all' (Head of English Department in a boys' grammar school).

Chapter Two

THEORY

TEACHERS' CRITERIA FOR THEIR CHOICE OF BOOKS

Despite the present vastly improved situation with regard to the availability of material I described earlier, the choice an individual teacher has in deciding what book best meets the needs of a particular class is, in fact, a limited one. I am very much aware that in asking teachers to select and describe their teaching methods with a book which they consider to have been successful, the teachers themselves have to make a choice from material, the original selection of which in turn has been affected by factors outside their direct control. The young teacher particularly may have little say in what books his department acquires, and the more senior teacher taking over a department is faced with a full stock cupboard of books provided by his predecessors. (In contrast some of the independent schools have a great advantage here in that the pupils themselves are expected to provide their own books.) Thus a number of teachers were anxious to make it very clear that their choice was based upon what they considered to be the best available to them in their particular school situation.

The other major factor affecting a teacher's choice of material at the upper end of the age-range we are concerned with is that the books to be read are chosen by external examiners. This affects every teacher concerned with G.C.E. 'O' level Literature and indeed many who are involved in C.S.E., but not working to a Mode 3 Syllabus. There are many examples of G.C.E. 'set books' being taught successfully, both in terms of the best kind of literature teaching and what the examiners require, but many of these teachers when interviewed agreed that they would not themselves have chosen to use the books which the examiners had foisted upon them.[1] One of the factors behind the noticeably wide currency of Golding's *Lord of the Flies* and Orwell's *Animal Farm* must be that both books are at present widely set by the G.C.E. examiners.[2]

However, even in cases where the teachers' initial choice was a limited one, most of the teachers I interviewed were fairly explicit about why they were using the books which they were using.

I have attempted to categorize the criteria which they produced, but inevitably these have to be fairly broad and it is perhaps dangerously misleading to isolate any of these criteria, without considering the implications for all the others.

A. *To Extend the Child's Experience and Knowledge of Life*

All the teachers interviewed produced this very basic criterion, some very explicitly, others implied it, but all considered it important. Most felt that any book which was to be used successfully and positively with adolescents must have an emotional appeal which allowed for identification and involvement in order to enrich their own experience of human behaviour and thus, mostly through discussion, to help them come to some sort of terms with themselves and society.

Moonfleet is a book which a number of teachers found successful with more junior forms. One saw it as an outstanding book for increasing understanding of human behaviour, another called it 'a microcosm of life'. More specifically, it shows very clearly that life is not a simple process of good versus evil, that moral values and human situations cannot be simply labelled black and white. Above all, 'it includes experiences which children ought to think about (e.g. death) in order that these may be better coped with in real life'.

Lord of the Flies is a book which many teachers found very valuable with rather older children for precisely the same

---

[1] See Chapter Six for a more detailed discussion of G.C.E. Literature.
[2] Far more questionnaires were returned about these two titles than any others.

kind of reason. A very lively and successful secondary modern teacher puts it thus: 'It gets them to see that a "rattling good yarn" can make a serious point about human behaviour. By exploiting their imaginative involvement to teach them certain important facts about human nature, i.e. that people fall out with one another, they project their fears on to bogeymen and scapegoats and they are subject to dangerous mass hysteria. . . . It is about situations and problems which play a large part in their experience.'

Another teacher used *Animal Farm* very deliberately because she felt that its different levels (e.g. the fable element) provided a very important bridge between child and adult experience.

Basically it's fidelity to human experience—this given in a form accessible to them. The animal-story form is accessible to most people—this age-group [intelligent fourteen-year-olds] is old enough to get the social and some of the political implications, yet young enough to associate themselves with an animal story. At this age they are partly living in two worlds— partly childhood where they might almost believe in Animals (temporarily as characters) and they are beginning to move in an adult world where perhaps they are beginning to see themselves as members of a society and becoming more objective.

Another teacher in a very different kind of school and dealing with younger children felt very similarly about *The Way of Danger*. The book provided 'a sufficient release from their own environment for a new enjoyment and yet a sufficient vocabulary and account of events for them not to feel that they are returning to a fantasy world or one of "Jack the Giant-killer"'. (Other books in which this kind of involvement at different levels was specifically mentioned were *Wuthering Heights*, *Short Stories of Our Time* and *Lord of the Flies*.)

A young teacher using *Short Stories of Our Time* in a school in a very deprived area put it very simply and specifically as follows:

1. It helps them to formulate things they've already thought about.
2. It lets them see that the same things happen to other people as to them.

11

3. It makes them think more deeply about things such as the woman next door.
4. I wanted them to try and gain more understanding of situations, instead of just accepting them.
5. I wanted them to be more subjective, for instance they could see a boy in America in the same situation as themselves, but it was not embarrassing to the children and did not say, 'Look! You are in the same situation.'
6. I hoped it would make them foresee problems before they happen—though that is most unlikely.
7. It helps them understand their own attitudes to things, e.g. 'Why do we want to stay out late?'
'Why do we want to drink or smoke?'

Some of the other teachers interviewed felt it important to put *all this* into a wider social and cultural context. A teacher using *The History of Mr Polly* wanted his children 'to see themselves as part of a tradition and culture. To relate it to their own families, parents, grandparents, etc.' He wanted them to taste the 'flavour of a couple of generations ago'. Others were very conscious of the position of 'Man in Society' with all that this implies socially, historically and politically. *The History of Mr Polly* was again mentioned specifically here, as were *Animal Farm* and *Lord of the Flies*. Others again were more directly anxious to awaken the social conscience of their pupils (*The Road to Wigan Pier*; *The Family from One End Street*; *The Mill on the Floss*; *Moonfleet*). Whatever other criteria they produced, almost every teacher interviewed made the point that they particularly wanted the children to appreciate the human relationships within the book.

However, some teachers were not only concerned to help their children to sift and evaluate their own experiences of life in the way just described, but also chose some books because they offered experiences far beyond those that most children would have personally encountered. *King Solomon's Mines* and *The Way of Danger* were specifically mentioned here, but this point of view was put most strongly and controversially by a teacher (in a girls' secondary modern school) in describing why she was using *Wuthering Heights*. 'You should never teach within the children's experience. We tend to be afraid that children can't appreciate beyond their own experience. I've never found this with literature, drama, or poetry—they can appreciate the best. We wanted something that took children away completely from their mundane ideas of life—so we gave them something that transcends the boundaries of life. I was determined that they were to have the fascination of the mystic everlasting quality of the book.'

A different kind of extension of the child's experience was looked for by those who were using good science fiction. Put bluntly, '*Brave New World* makes them sit up and think'; or as a teacher using Ray Bradbury's *The Day it Rained for Ever* said, 'It introduces new concepts in a way which children can assimilate with assistance, thus giving rise to more interesting discussion; because many of our preconceived concepts are ignored in the stories—to allow growth of ideas and questioning of established attitudes through class discussion of the book.' This seems to me one of the most important criteria produced by any of the teachers interviewed, in that so many other educational, social, political and economic pressures are concerned with making the child conform to an established pattern of behaviour and with fitting him for a pre-determined role in society.

B. *To Help the Child's Personal Growth*
Most of the teachers I interviewed showed some awareness of the psychological needs of developing adolescents and indeed this is implicit in some of the statements already quoted. However, there were some who clearly placed a more central emphasis upon this criterion than did others, or at least they stated it much more explicitly. They felt that self-identification in order to assist in maturation and self-adjustment was important. A comprehensive school teacher thought this the most valuable element in *Lord of the Flies*. 'It is an allegory, allowing identification. They can see the types among their own fellows. [There is] a hell of a lot to talk about in its relevance to their development as children of this age. The third year age—a turmoil of adolescence—anything that helps them to get guide lines [is] important. Psychologically [it is] a matter of recognition of factors inside themselves. Recognition [is] half the

battle in controlling them.' The teacher already quoted in talking about the new concepts raised by *The Day it Rained for Ever* went on to explain the success of the book in these terms:

Self-identification is reasonably easy. [The] majority of characters, good and sordid, do or say something which rouses empathy in the children. The words and actions are not always those they expect to hear read out in the classroom and sometimes put the character in a dilemma which the child himself may appreciate. Self-identification is important as you get their attention better and they have dozens of problems themselves which they are incapable, often owing to [the] hostility of their contemporaries, of expressing or releasing. Some of them are touched on in the book, e.g. loneliness, boredom, a feeling of being different and of not wanting to conform.

Other teachers implied that they were consciously using literature to help their children with their own problems of development, in a more personal sense, than those whose criteria were, broadly speaking, 'social'. Like those teachers using a 'social' criterion, they wanted the books to assist the children in their growing understanding of human behaviour, and of other people, and to apply what they learned to their own situations, but in a much more subjective sense and as a more conscious aid to personal maturity. Books found particularly useful for this were: *Tom Sawyer* (with very specific reference to boy/girl relationships); *A Sillitoe Selection* (a coming to terms with rebelliousness); *The Children* or *Walkabout* (which several teachers found valuable because it raised very sensitively and sensibly the whole issue of the growing awareness of sexual relationships).

C. *Qualities of the Book which Appeal to Children*
Whatever other criteria were produced, there was a universal concern that the children should enjoy the books which were read. As one would expect, the reasons which teachers gave for the appeal of a given book to their own pupils varied very greatly according to their own particular teaching situation.
Some, especially teachers of more 'difficult' children, were

concerned that the story should be exciting in a way which provides a focal point for the class's attention. *Lord of the Flies* was mentioned several times in this connection and *The Otterbury Incident* and *Night Cargoes* were also specifically picked out. I have already briefly noted the different levels of appreciation which are possible when reading *Animal Farm*. Another secondary modern teacher found that his children experienced in this book something rather deeper than the superficial excitement or element of surprise in a good story well told. 'The excitement of an unfolding significance—a time bomb effect of it gradually dawning on the children that it isn't really about animals.'

Those who taught children who were culturally deprived, whose sole 'literary' experience outside school was probably limited to reading comics and watching television, sometimes felt that the choice of any book which their children could enjoy would have to take this into account. Thus one teacher using *King Solomon's Mines* with a particularly deprived class felt that it was successful because it is 'an adventure story—a bravado expedition similar to what they have an interest in from comics and TV. It has the same qualities in a good literary form.' Another secondary modern teacher, using what most of us would agree to be a book far more worth using— *Tom Sawyer*—found that it 'appeals to the *Comic Cuts* idea—you can bridge the *Tom Sawyer–Beano* gap. There are so many facets feeding into the central theme, i.e. from the *Beano* at one extreme to young love at the other.' The same teacher also felt that a book about troublesome boys had a particular appeal to troublesome boys, and more positively it provided an opportunity to talk about authority and how they saw themselves in relation to it.

Similarly, those teaching girls sometimes emphasized the particular appeal to them of books about children or a domestic situation (*A Waltz Through the Hills*, *Silas Marner*). Others stressed the appeal of the theme of courtship—often comparable with their own experiences in the case of the older girls (*Far from the Madding Crowd*, *Geordie*). The interest of adolescents in boy/girl relationships was also mentioned (*The Children*, *A Kind of Loving*). Others felt strongly about the

15

appeal of a story about children to children of a similar age (*Moonfleet, Lord of the Flies, There Is a Happy Land*).

Humour was sometimes felt to be an important ingredient in books which children enjoyed. It was mentioned very specifically in connection with *The History of Mr Polly, Animal Farm, There Is a Happy Land* and *The Children*—interestingly, books which have all been previously mentioned for other reasons.

Some teachers tended to fe ' that it was very helpful if the book had an episodic quality and thus could naturally be broken down into sections and considered a bit at a time (e.g. *Way of Danger* and *Pilgrim's Progress* lent themselves well to this kind of treatment with lower forms; *The Pickwick Papers* and *The History of Mr Polly* with older children). Others, and particularly those not concerned with the ablest children, were strong advocates of the short story for much the same reasons. *Short Stories of Our Time, Short Stories for Girls* and *Facing Facts* were felt to be particularly useful. They were enjoyed because of the appeal of the contemporary language and situations; and they were useful because they gave the experience of very different types of writing fairly painlessly and led the children on to novels.

Some of the teachers interviewed were also very conscious of the importance of the language and style of the books they used in considering their appeal to the children. *Facing Facts*, for instance, was not only successful for the reason described above, but was 'linguistically easy to get at'. *The Way of Danger* and *Men and Gods* were felt to be successful with lower forms 'because it frees them [i.e. the children] from the demands of language used in many novels based on classical stories'. These teachers were concerned that the books they used made 'clear statements' (both in terms of content and language structure) and that they were 'written in comprehensible language using terms that they [the children] understand'. *The Day it Rained for Ever, Five Children and It, Bitter Herbs, Animal Farm, Lord of the Flies, A Sillitoe Selection* were all judged successful from this point of view. In contrast, one highly intelligent class of boys particularly enjoyed *The History of Mr Polly*, because of the playing with words and language patterns which the book offered.

Any book chosen, however carefully and for whatever qualities it possesses, will clearly not appeal to all members of a class to the same degree, and as adolescence progresses this becomes particularly true of mixed classes. However, my testing of some children's reactions to some books (Appendix A) shows quite clearly that at least with these books and these classes, most of the children were enjoying the books they were reading. Further, although boys and girls reacted differently in mixed classes, the total reaction of boys and girls separately to the books they were reading was remarkably similar.

My own teaching experience with all kinds of children leads me to believe that the right material of the right quality produces a situation where, although some children enjoy a particular book more than others, all the individual responses are positive and differ only in degree.

D. *The Appeal of the Book to the Teacher*
Some teachers felt that they could only successfully use books which they reacted to strongly themselves, and most experienced teachers of English would agree that this kind of enthusiasm and joy in reading is infectious. One outstanding teacher I interviewed had fairly recently 'discovered' Thornton Wilder's *The Ides of March*. 'It has tremendous range. It is marvellous in the way it is done as an imaginative reconstruction of Caesar's Rome, all kinds of evidence is used to build up the total picture —from the scavenger to the lady-in-waiting. It has an almost Shakespearian range. One or two rather enigmatic characters emerge. There is an interesting comparison to be drawn between Caesar's public and private lives. One gets a great sense of depth, of the complexity of any given situation—almost Tolstoyan. The book does have extreme depth and perception which makes it certainly the best thing Wilder has ever written.' He went on to say that he had come across the book in the school holidays and could hardly wait for the term to begin before getting at it with the children (it was used most effectively as part of a G.C.E. course in which *Julius Caesar* was the set Shakespearian text).

Another teacher in a very different kind of school felt equally strongly about *Wuthering Heights*. 'It has a perpetual quality . . . it is a book with a force and depth that is utterly absorbing.'

Clearly these teachers are, consciously or unconsciously, making their own response to literature one of the criteria by which they choose books for their children. The same point was made, not often so coherently or in such detail, by a number of other teachers I interviewed.

A retrospective response of perhaps not quite the same kind was made by some teachers who admitted that they wanted their children to enjoy the book in the same way that they had themselves enjoyed it as children.

E. *The Use of the Book as a Basis for Other 'English' Activities*
Many teachers also chose the book they were using because they felt that it had a particular value in relation to some other area of English teaching.

Some were anxious for their pupils to be faced with a model of 'good writing'. In discussing *Men and Gods*, one teacher said that she wanted to help them to be aware of the quality of words and of the importance of precise detail. Another found *Facing Facts* a useful book for discussing and demonstrating the relevance of significant detail in short-story writing. Others wanted to use a book which served as an example of a particular style of writing or alternatively showed a versatility of style. (Books mentioned specifically here were: *Tom Sawyer, Short Stories of Our Time, The Road to Wigan Pier, Lord of the Flies, A Sillitoe Selection, Moonfleet*.) Sometimes this was required for Comprehension work, e.g. 'There are specific passages of value for their own content which are extractable and can be used in isolation' (*King Solomon's Mines, Tom Sawyer*); sometimes as an example, e.g. 'of excellent descriptive writing' (*Moonfleet*), and sometimes more specifically in connection with the child's own writing ('it helps fluency in essay writing to have studied the development of a story').

However, despite the concern of some to provide their children with a 'model', most of the teachers interviewed were more concerned to use the book as the basis for creative written work of all kinds. 'I hoped they would begin to write the same sort of thing as Wilder by seeing things through others' eyes' (this is very different from using Wilder as a model in a stylistic sense). Other books which were found to be valuable as a springboard for creative written work were: *A Waltz Through the Hills, Tom Sawyer, Animal Farm*. The Day it *Rained for Ever* provided all kinds of stimuli for writing, especially when used in conjunction with poetry (Eliot's 'The River is within us', Graves' 'Children if you dare to think', MacNeice's 'Prayer before Birth' were specifically mentioned).

Some teachers also implied that the success of a book was often dependent upon its potential for classroom drama. *Lord of the Flies* was mentioned several times in this context and I came across instances of *Moonfleet, The History of Mr Polly, Pilgrim's Progress, Men and Gods* and *The Wind in the Willows* giving rise to worthwhile and creative dramatic work. After giving a very effective drama lesson with a first-year class of secondary modern girls, based on *The Way of Danger*, the teacher commented; 'It gives them the core of the story, leaving out the detail, which at the beginning of the school year with a new teacher may become tedious. The first stages over, it allows for the introduction of parallel characters of much greater depth, for example Lady Macbeth was introduced by reference to Medea. It gave them a chance to expand the characters in their own way in drama groups, it allowed us to put them in slightly foreign situations, e.g. Darkness for the Underworld. It allowed them to create scenes in drama and writing which relied on recapitulation of events.'

Thus, by working through drama this teacher led her children from Medea, at a fairly unsophisticated level, eventually to Lady Macbeth. There were other teachers who were similarly anxious that their choice of reading material should not be seen in isolation, and who stressed its links with other literature of all kinds. One secondary modern teacher was reading *Animal Farm* and *Lord of the Flies* at the same time because with a parallel approach they dovetailed well together. They had certain problems in common and from the practical teaching point of view much preparation work could apply equally to either book. Sometimes the link was through language; one teacher made the point that the poetic qualities of *Wuthering Heights* made many cross-references to poetry and drama possible, and we have already noted how another teacher used poetry in connection with *The Day it Rained for Ever* to provide a stimulus for writing. Others saw the book they were concerned with at the moment as part of a much wider context in a thematic sense.

Thus a teacher dealing with the theme of 'Growing Up' was at the time I interviewed her basically using *A Waltz Through the Hills*, but also mentioned *The Yearling, Great Expectations, To Kill a Mocking Bird, The Diary of Anne Frank* and *Lord of the Flies*, with which the children could all eventually be involved in one way or another. Similarly, those using books of short stories almost always made the point that the stories within the volume were not considered in isolation, but always in relation to each other.

A few teachers had the needs of oral English particularly in mind. One teacher with a first-year secondary modern class used *Five Children and It*, partly because it gave her comparatively young children easy practice in reading aloud. A boys' grammar school, in whose syllabus Spoken English played a far larger and more central part than is usual, used carefully selected extracts from *The Thurber Carnival* not only as an introduction to the literary form of the fable and short story as such, but also as leading to the recognition of a literary form eminently suitable for speaking aloud and from which could be developed a story-telling (N.B. not writing) technique.

F. 'Literary' Criteria

Some teachers (and they were not always those with the most sensitive and responsive pupils) were concerned to deepen their pupils' literary awareness and aesthetic appreciation of literature. As one teacher using *Animal Farm* put it, she wanted her pupils to be 'sensitive to a mode of conveying human experience in art'.

Others were very much aware that reading in depth had to be taught. A grammar school teacher aimed 'to encourage the pupils to read more deeply (looking for implications) and to assist in discernment because they won't always be reading superficially. Looking for depths in a book is a skill that is learned.' This point was made several times in discussing *Lord of the Flies* and was also sometimes made specifically when discussing rather younger classes, especially in connection with *The Pearl* and *Pilgrim's Progress*.

Some teachers wanted their books to provide an opportunity for the teaching and study of 'literary appreciation'. They were far more concerned than were most others with the problems of character analysis, the inter-relationship of characters, the effect of the environment on the individual (in a literary rather than a social sense), irony, points of style, etc. Others felt that in order to further literary appreciation it was important to consider and recognize such features as symbolism and allegory, and used books such as *Animal Farm, Pilgrim's Progress* and *Men and Gods* to teach these terms.

This approach to literature teaching would seem to me of value only if the object of such 'literary' considerations is to assist in the realization of some of the other criteria I have already discussed, and particularly the first two. Provided that this is clearly the intention, it may be of some value for more intelligent children. It would, however, seem to be of no value for the more average and less able children, and indeed a completely misconceived approach to literature with any child if it is regarded as an end in itself or allowed to play a central role in any conception of literature teaching.

I have already mentioned *Short Stories of Our Time* in discussing other criteria. Clearly the teacher who said about this book 'The standard of writing is such that close analysis is profitable' is looking at it rather differently, although he did go on to say that it 'introduces well-known authors by lesser-known works and leads [the children] hopefully to read their better-known works'.

This last point, i.e. that the book stimulates further reading of a similar 'good' quality, although infrequently stated as a criterion of choice, was implied and assumed in the majority of interviews. It was stated quite explicitly in discussing *Short Stories of Our Time* (as I have just noted) and *Moonfleet, King Solomon's Mines, The Road to Wigan Pier* and *The Pickwick Papers*. This seems to me to be an assumption that we have all made for too long and is clearly so common that it is time it was proved!

The criteria discussed above are inter-related in complex ways, and most teachers clearly base their work on a combination of certain of them. They all, however, have one clear factor in common. The implementation of these criteria has caused the teachers to undertake a variety of activities which are not only firmly based upon the book in question, but also upon the common experience and involvement of the whole class. This in turn has led to a conscious need for, and choice of, a class set of books. The Head of the English Department in a girls' grammar school said to me, 'I feel more and more that I want to base what I do in English on the basic symbols and experiences of the human race. At the same time I don't want to lose sight of the uniqueness of the books themselves.' The class reader has a unique part to play in achieving this aim.

A DISSENTING VIEW

However, the view I have so far expressed is not one that would be shared by all English teachers. A small number of teachers reported that they were unable to complete my questionnaire as they would never consider using a class reader. They argue that in any class 'tastes, abilities and responses vary so much that the use of a "class reader" in any form is largely a waste of time!' and that 'the forced study of any one book produced a negative reaction from at least half the class'. The responses of the children to my five-point rating scale in the schools that were visited would not support this view (see Appendix A). They also argue that the practical difficulties involved in using a common book which children read at very different speeds and with varying enthusiasm are insurmountable, but tend to ignore the fact that individual reading schemes produce practical problems of their own. One supporter of exclusively individual reading spoke of his difficulties when a book suddenly became so popular with a class that it gave rise to spontaneous and valuable classroom discussion, but it was then difficult quickly to obtain enough copies of the book in question. Many of the supporters of the class reader spoke of the many practical difficulties involved in ensuring that all the children in the class were getting all that they should from an

individual reader and in planning any effective follow-up work or activity upon an individual basis. Teachers using individual readers exclusively reported on such follow-up activities as personal reporting, dramatization, tape-recorded versions of episodes, etc.; I would argue that such projects would be more valuable if the whole class had had the experience of the original book first.

It was also very noticeable that those teachers advocating exclusively individual reading did in fact need to provide their classes with a common experience in other ways. Particularly mentioned were B.B.C. School Broadcasts (*Living Language*; *Listening and Writing*; *Drama Workshop*; *Speak*; *Books, Plays, Poems*); libraries of tape-recordings; records of literary material; and the reading to the class of extracts from books of all kinds. It seems absurdly illogical to argue that thirty individual children cannot benefit from the experience of the same book, but can gain something from the experience of the same broadcast or recording.

It seems quite clear that for some teachers the very term 'class reader' is a loaded one. It was noticeable that some of the teachers I interviewed in depth, and who supported the use of the class reader, were unnecessarily defensive until reassured that I was making no preliminary assumptions; however, those who oppose the use of the class reader make a great many assumptions, most of them emotional rather than rational. It is assumed that the use of a class reader can only mean 'reading round the class' or close textual analysis of the G.C.E. kind. The language used in discussing the whole issue is emotively biased—witness such terms as 'set book' or even 'prose indoctrination'. As a further example, consider the assumptions underlying the following statement! 'The aim [i.e. of individual reading] is to encourage reading for enjoyment and at this early stage a close study of a book along the lines of the familiar "O" level approach would, with the type of children I teach [secondary modern], have a distinctly "off-putting" effect.'

It is difficult to estimate how widespread the reaction against the class reader is. The number of teachers who supported schemes of exclusively individual reading and who reported to

me was very much smaller than the number who reported on the successful use of a class reader. Clearly, however, there may be a much larger number who, feeling that they were not in a position to answer my questionnaire, did not report to me at all.[1] Two trends are discernible among those who did. Firstly, as I have briefly shown, they felt very strongly opposed to the use of the class reader at all, secondly they nearly all taught at highly selective grammar or independent schools.

It cannot be too strongly emphasized that the teachers who support the use of the class reader also encourage, support and make use of individual reading schemes of all kinds. They would add, however, that the proper use of the class text has a unique place in their teaching. It is to a detailed consideration of that place that we now turn.

[1] The University of Newcastle upon Tyne Institute of Education's survey into the teaching of English in local secondary schools (1964) concluded that, in the North-East at least, teachers still seemed to rely fairly heavily on 'class sets' of prose readers.

Chapter Three

PRACTICE

Whereas in the previous chapter we touched briefly on many different books, it seemed to me that in turning now to consider actual classroom practices we ought to look hard at a few books, in order to focus our thinking and to provide specific and detailed examples. The six books discussed in this chapter and the next are therefore representative of the kind of practice reported upon by a great many teachers about a great many books. These particular books were chosen for one of two reasons: either they are books which were in wide use and therefore about which quite a lot of specific information was forthcoming, or they are books which provided outstandingly interesting examples of ways in which a book can be used with particular children. I was most anxious, for instance, to discover and record examples of good practice in the teaching of less able children. It also seemed to me important to discuss examples covering the whole of the age and ability range with which the Project was concerned.

Thus, the four main examples are arranged roughly in the age order of the classes with which the book was in use, beginning with the youngest. The last two examples are concerned very specifically with less able children of very different ages.

MOONFLEET
J. Meade Falkner. (Edward Arnold—Arnold's English Literature Series—or Puffin Books—Penguin)
Age-range: 12–14

This book had a universal appeal within this age-range and was successfully used in every type of school, in mixed and

25

single-sex, streamed and unstreamed classes throughout the full normal-ability range.

A teacher in a fairly small, fairly remote secondary modern school thought that 'without exception [it is a book which appeals to both boys and girls] it is quite the most satisfactory reading book I have ever used'. Someone else, working in a very different environment (girls' London comprehensive), noted that 'This proved an absorbing story for the class [bright thirteen-year-old girls]; in spite of the fact that some girls are already beginning to become sophisticated.' Again, it was found an ideal choice for unstreamed classes. One very large mixed grammar school had conducted its own survey into the popularity of the books they were using. Questionnaires were completed by all classes from the second year up to and including the fifth year—nearly forty per cent of the children cited *Moonfleet* as the book they had most enjoyed reading during their years in the school.

One does not have to look very far for the reasons for this popularity. As one grammar school teacher put it, 'This book is not a particularly good one, but like the average "Western", it appeals to the entire range of ability.' I take his point, although he and I would not agree about the literary merits of the book; nor do I think that the average 'Western' contains anything like the same qualities of compassion or insight into human behaviour. However, purely at the level of adventure, 'It has all the features likely to appeal to the thirteen/fourteen year age-groups: a search for treasure: the macabre (in the vault); danger and escape: the efforts of one boy on his own to come to grips with his environment, and some romantic interest' (secondary modern school). Or again: 'I found this book particularly suitable for reading by a whole class at this age [thirteen-plus] as there are so many passages of strong dramatic interest—the selling of the lease of the Inn—the trapping of the boy in the vault—the flight from the soldiers and the climbing of the cliff—the cracking of Blackbeard's code—the episode in the well house, etc.' (bilateral school).

These are the qualities which account for the book's popularity among children, the qualities of the average 'Western', if you like. It does, however, offer a great deal more from the teaching point of view. A secondary modern teacher I interviewed, after discussing the interest of the book for the kinds of reasons mentioned above, went on to say: 'More important, however, it offers so much scope for the exploration of human experience, and the discussion of moral issues and judgements. While the ingredients of romance, adventure, pathos, tragedy and suspense are all present, the child can see the relevance of the situations in which the characters find themselves and the emotions they feel, and recognize that they are akin to his own experience.' Any teacher using the book without taking these qualities into account is mis-using it.

I have already discussed in general terms both the reciprocal process and the shared experience which the use of a good class reader can offer. A secondary modern teacher put this very specifically when discussing *Moonfleet*, and again this would in part account for the book's success.

This is a story which can be enjoyed by the children at their own level and by many teachers at an adult level. This is important because the children soon sense the fact if the teacher is bored. The interest of one party stimulates that of the other. Moreover, as the confidence of the children increases with the former's consciousness of a *shared* enjoyment, it becomes possible for the teacher to lead the children to glimpse some of the enjoyment possible at his own level, e.g. the greater effectiveness of Block as a boy's guardian compared with Aunt Jane; the 'sublimating' influence of an innocent boy and girl friendship; the quiet wisdom of Mr Glennie. Here of course the discussion reaches well beyond the frontiers of the book into contemporary experience. It was possible to convince the class (or, better still, allow them to convince you) that the more plausible characters and situations are, the more the story can be enjoyed and the more it relates to life, i.e. it is not merely escapist. This was done by comparing the book with certain TV programmes, e.g. *The Avengers* or *Dr Who*.

Treatment of the Book

A. Discussion

The book provided the teachers who were using it with many and far-ranging topics for discussion. Most of these were concerned with background information relating to the book and aspects of 'general knowledge' arising from it. This kind of discussion included such topics as smuggling and the contemporary attitude to it, the influence formerly exercised by prominent local families in rural districts, Crown Lands, diamonds as a form of permanent wealth, the severity of the criminal code of the period compared with our attitude today. Such class discussion seems to me completely justifiable in so far as it is necessary to a particular class's understanding of the book and if it leads spontaneously to the exploration of issues which are of genuine concern to the children. I would argue, however, that when such topics grow into separate and independent projects of their own we are leading the children away from what the book is really about.

In one particular case the school was situated very close to the sea, the relatives of many of the children earned their living from it and the whole area was still soaked in smuggling lore. Here the children spent quite a lot of time giving talks about and discussing the smuggling tales still extant in the district.

For this school and for these children, smuggling was understandably and rightly one of the central issues of the book, but for schools not similarly placed I would argue that those teachers using the book as a basis for a topic on smuggling (or anything else!) are as mistaken as those who treat it as a pure adventure story.

As I have already argued, it is the human relationships and experience within this book that are crucial and that ought to be central to all class discussion. As one teacher wrote in describing the discussion arising from the book:

The class found the human relationships in the story moving and credible—the Aunt's rejection of the boy, Elzevir's acceptance and substitution of him for his dead son, and the boy's affection for Grace Maskell and his respect for her feelings for her father who was universally disliked—these [were] all discussed and justified with examples of the same thing or [the] opposite quoted from their [the children's] own experiences . . . it gave rise to much discussion and self-searching, e.g. with regard to moral and political attitudes.

28

It is not always necessary to hold a complete class discussion. One secondary modern teacher sometimes held discussions in groups; group leaders reported the main points of the discussion to the rest of the class and summarized the group's views and conclusions. Some of the issues successfully discussed in this way were:

(a) Whether smuggling could be justified—whether Elzevir was really a 'criminal'—whether obeying the law makes a person 'good'.
(b) Whether revenge is ever justified—whether Elzevir would have been justified in shooting Maskew,
(c) Is Elzevir wiser than John in thinking John greedy?
(d) Is John greedy?

B. Characterization

Some teachers approached the book very much through the characters in the story. To one, the book's appeal lay in the 'accurate portrayal of very convincing characters, going through experiences which the children ought to think about, e.g. the death of Elzevir—girl in class in similar situation. [They are] better able to cope with these experiences in real life, having met them in literature.'

One grammar school teacher tied his consideration of the characters very firmly to the moral issues which the book raises. 'My main hope was that they would see the importance of characterization and recognize that characters do not fall into simple categories of black and white. This emerged very quickly as regards Elzevir after we had read *in class* the opening two chapters. John's "greyness" emerged later and it was interesting to note how at times the class shrank from involvement with him.' This conscious detachment here is noteworthy—most of the boys who were reading the book identified very strongly throughout with John Trenchard.

C. Written Work

The following are examples of some of the kinds of written work successfully undertaken with the book.

1. *Written work remaining within the experience of the book*
(*a*) Relating an episode specifically from the point of view of one of the characters. e.g. (i) John Trenchard tells of his experiences in the vault, this sometimes followed by an attempt to imagine how he made his escape (before that part of the story was read), or (ii) Maskew tells of how he was captured and killed.
(*b*) In one lesson which I observed the teacher led the class through reading and discussion to the point where John was looking at Elzevir's half-naked corpse on the beach. The children were reminded of all the varied experiences which the two characters had shared and asked to write down what John was thinking—a series of thoughts in sentence form or 'free verse if you like'—'Choose a title which suits the mood of your writing best'. Another alternative was 'Put yourselves into the position of John Trenchard, sitting near Elzevir's grave two or three years later. What are his thoughts?'

2. *Written work starting within the experience of the book and then moving outside it into other kinds of related experience*
Opportunities are given to the class 'to describe experiences similar to John's, e.g. of momentary horror, or suspense, of realization, of fear, of being rescued from danger. Attempts are encouraged to describe in minute detail such familiar scenes and experiences as John's bedroom when the house is quiet or the interior of the Church on a wet Sunday morning. The background and starting point of the familiar is often what makes the horror, or suspense, or heroic, more convincing.' Other examples were: 'Write about a time when you had an opportunity for taking revenge (cf. Maskew at the mercy of Elzevir); write about a moment of bitter disappointment (cf. Elzevir's loss of the "Why Not?" and later when he and John were told that the jewel was worthless).' And again: 'After reading how John Trenchard discovered Blackbeard's diamond (Chapter Fifteen), illustrations of great diamonds and of diamond-cutters were passed round the class. The resulting poems showed that many of the boys and girls appreciated both the obvious beauty of the gem-stones and

their less obvious power to corrupt by encouraging man's greed for wealth.'

3. *Written work allied specifically to the use of a tape-recorder*
(*a*) The writing of scripts for 'radio', e.g. The Auction, The Interview. Individual work on scripts was followed by group reading of scripts. Each group selected the best script and prepared it for recording on tape (this also involved the preparation of reading 'in character', the noting and experimenting with sound effects and the successful cueing in of these).
(*b*) Written interviews with characters in the story—these also were tape-recorded.

D. Drama

Another teacher I interviewed used a tape-recorder no less successfully, but rather differently. The original dialogue of the book was retained and 'parts of *Moonfleet* were taped—I acted as narrator and the children spoke the dialogue. This proved particularly effective in their Cornish dialect—exaggerated by some to befit the occasion!' The same teacher went on to say that 'From the point of view of drama—this particular type of book for this particular type of class (mixed secondary modern fourteen-plus lowish stream) was good. They were able to make exhibitions of themselves but because this was down to earth and near home they were prepared to act. We didn't bother about the book. Because the smugglers were very down to earth, they could cope with it and they enjoyed doing it.'

Another secondary modern teacher described his drama work with the book rather more specifically as follows:

Following the reading of the episodes which lend themselves to dramatization, character and situation would be discussed, the essential action noted and an improvised 'set' planned. Properties essential to the action would be acquired (frequently improvised) and volunteers asked for. This group would then improvise the scene. Follow-up would include critical comment—what succeeded? what failed? More specific questioning would elicit comment on how far the characters succeeded in showing emotion (by gesture, voice, etc.), whether the dialogue was convincing and so on. Other teams of pupils might then act their versions of the scene. Episodes which were worked on in this way were: The Auction, The Capture and Death of Maskew, and the Jewel incident at Aldobrand's house.

E. Language Work and Structure of the Book

One grammar school is so situated that Moonfleet Bay and Beach can actually be seen from the classroom windows and the remains of Fleet Church are within a mile's walk of the school. This school showed more concern than most with the language of the book. 'We suggest that they [the children] look for the climax of a passage and trace how Meade Falkner leads up to it, building with words the impression and atmosphere he wishes to create, e.g. "horror"—in the Sea Cave; dizziness and fear—the climb up Hoar Head.'

This kind of language analysis is quite common, particularly amongst teachers concerned with more able children. However, the chief reason for their concern with language was more unusual and arose directly from their living within the 'setting' of *Moonfleet*. They were anxious that their children learned 'to see, hear and appreciate the true nature of their environment', which was the environment of *Moonfleet*. They trained their children to look for what they called 'true flash pictures' in words, in simile or metaphor, e.g. the rooks 'pitch-falling before a gale, the moving floor of the channel beneath'. 'The straight sun-path across it, gleaming and spangled like a mackerel's back.'

Thus the children became more observant of their environment and tried 'to clothe their [own] thoughts in more vivid, or lucid, or aptly chosen words'.

The same school was also concerned with the structure of the book in a way in which most others were not. 'As we read on, we follow the mentions of the "object clues" as they occur, e.g. Maskew's silver-butted pistol, John's mother's red prayer book, and Blackbeard's diamond. We trace the significance of Ratsey's work as parish mason, clerk and sexton, and of Grace Maskew's words, "It was evilly come by and will bring evil with it." So a sense of logical sequence is developed.'

F. A Complete Term's Work

I have discussed earlier the possibility of using the class reader as a kind of framework within which to operate and as a way of giving a sense of unity to all 'English' activities.

I am most grateful to one of the teachers I interviewed for allowing me to reproduce both his term's scheme of work based upon *Moonfleet* and his detailed account of how the book was subsequently taught. I would like to emphasize the very careful preliminary planning which took place. As he himself described it:

Before setting out to teach from this novel some consider-able preparation had to be done. On re-reading it I was able to draw up a scheme of English work based on a passage or passages from each chapter of the book. These passages can be used for teaching to various ranges of ability for they include straightforward descriptions of scenery, incidents and people, dialogue, characterization and the play of character upon character. I then selected the material that would be relevant and suitable for the age-group I was to teach (eleven/twelve-year-old boys). Having done this I divided the material under two main headings: Material for Creative Writing and Material for Discussion, Material for Impromptu Drama. The material for Creative Writing was then graded so that at the beginning of term descriptive writing of scenery could be taught, in which the class would be encouraged to use all their five senses; later the description of dramatic incidents was taught; then characterization by describing appearance, habits, thoughts and by writing dialogue. The material for discussion was divided according to themes such as Fear, Forgiveness, Greed, Self-Sacrifice. Finally two incidents in the novel, most dramatic in content and suitable for the classroom drama, were selected for improvisation.

THE SCHEME OF WORK *(Designed for 11/12-year-old boys)*

A. WRITING OR TALKING POINTS

1. *Moonfleet village (October evening 1787)*
   (Chapter I, pp. 9–11[1])

   (a) Describe $\begin{matrix} \text{an English} \\ \text{any} \end{matrix}$ village to day in $\begin{matrix} \text{Spring.} \\ \text{Summer.} \\ \text{Autumn.} \\ \text{Winter.} \end{matrix}$

   (b) Describe a familiar room in your own or someone else's house.

   (c) What is the worst dream you have ever had?

   (d) You enter a churchyard and find an old tombstone. You read what is written on it and reconstruct the life of the person buried there.

2. *The Storm (Chapter II, pp. 21–23). The Floods*

   (a) Describe a storm at sea or on land.

   (b) (pp. 23–25) Describe any church or cathedral you have visited. What effect does the building have on you?

   (c) (pp. 30–32) You have overheard an odd conversation or seen two people who are your friends acting strangely. Describe this and try to account for their words or actions.

3. *The Discovery (Chapter III)*

   (a) You are sitting in a favourite spot on a fine day and can see to quite a distance. What can you see, hear, feel, smell, taste?

   (b) (pp. 38–40) Describe any midnight adventure—real or imaginary—of your own.

4. *In the Vault (Chapter IV)*

   (a) (p. 50) Describe the approach of John as if he were in fact a spy or informer.

   (b) Describe a meeting at which you are a silent and concealed observer.

   (c) Describe any situation in which you were very afraid.

   (d) Imagine that you are exploring a cave when a sudden fall of earth entombs you. Describe your feelings and your efforts to get out.

[1] Page references refer to the Edward Arnold edition.

5. *An Assault (Chapter VI)*
    (*a*) Describe any derelict or deserted house you have seen or can imagine (p. 71).
    (*b*) Describe any situation in which you have felt embarrassed.
    (*c*) Describe any room in this school.
    (*d*) Describe a spendthrift, schoolmaster, generous man.
    (*e*) 'Not in front of the children.'

6. *The Auction (Chapter VII)*
    (*a*) Describe the interior of the 'Why Not?'.
    (*b*) Describe an occasion when you were bitterly disappointed because something that you had expected to happen had failed to happen.
    (*c*) What would it be like suddenly to lose your home?

7. *The Landing (Chapter VIII)*
    (*a*) Describe a walk or ride by night.
    (*b*) What would it feel like to see a friend or relative abused and assaulted.
    (*c*) Describe the feelings of a man who has done something despicable and is found out.

8. *The Skirmish (Chapter IX)*
    (*a*) Describe the life and death of a coward and a brave man.
    (*b*) Describe a skirmish with the enemy (past or present).

9. *The Escape (Chapter X)*
    (*a*) Describe the most dangerous thing (real or imaginary) that you have ever done.
    (*b*) Describe a steep climb or other similar experience in which all the muscles had to be used.
    (*c*) Describe a wounded man escaping across country and finding refuge—on the run.

10. *The Cryptogram (Chapter XII)*
    Make up your own cryptogram.

11. *Finding the Jewel (Chapters XIV and XV)*
    (*a*) Describe the finding of something of great value.
    (*b*) Describe any castle or fort that you have visited.
    (*c*) You are disguised. Describe your feelings as you slip through those who are trying to stop you.

35

12. *Arrest and Imprisonment (Chapters XVI and XVII)*
    (*a*) Describe a jewel robbery and the arrest of the thieves.
    (*b*) Describe a day in prison—dreams—reality.
    (*c*) Describe an escape from prison.

13. *The Shipwreck (Chapter XVIII)*
    (*a*) Describe a struggle for life.
    (*b*) Describe an accident in which life is endangered.
    (*c*) A last-minute rescue.

14. *On the Beach (Chapter XIX)*
    (*a*) Describe a return to the place where you once lived, happy or sad.
    (*b*) Describe the feelings of a man whose friend has given his life to save him.

B. CHARACTERS

1. *Aunt Jane*
   (*a*) What was her attitude to John?
   (*b*) Was it in any way justified?
       (pp. 9, 10, 36, 69, 243)

2. *Elzevir Block*
   (*a*) What was his attitude to John?
   (*b*) Would he have been justified in shooting Maskew?
   (*c*) Was he justified in killing the turnkey?

3. *David Block*
   Describe David Block as seen by John Trenchard.

4. *Maskew*
   (*a*) Was his conduct in any way justified? (Chapter VI).
   (*b*) What would it be like to have a father who was hated by everyone?

5. *Mr Glennie*
   (*a*) Describe a clergyman or schoolmaster whom you know.
   (*b*) What was Mr Glennie's attitude to the smugglers?
   (*c*) Should he have stood up for himself against Maskew?

6. *Ratsey*
   Describe a village craftsman at work.

C. REPORTING (WRITTEN AND ORAL)

Describe the school crest (the Mohune Shield, p. 14).

D. DRAMA

1. Improvise a scene from *Moonfleet*.
   (*a*) The adventure in the vault.
   (*b*) The meeting with the farmer's boy.
   (*c*) The skirmish and escape up the cliff.
   (*d*) The attempt to seize the diamond.
   (*e*) The shipwreck and rescue.
   (*f*) The shooting of David Block.
   (*g*) The auction of the 'Why Not?'.

2. Improvise a modern play about smuggling.

E. DISCUSSION

Forgiveness—Maskew's funeral. (Grace Maskew alone. Should the villagers, now the man was dead, have refrained from jeering and helped bury him?) 'Life is like a game of hazard; the skilful player will make something of the worst of throws.'

Two aspects of this scheme of work are worthy of comment: Firstly, the thoroughness and detail with which it has been worked out, well *before* the children have begun to read the book. Secondly, as the teacher himself points out, his writing and talking points include descriptive writing of all kinds, consideration of character and dialogue, and more purely imaginative or creative kinds of work. While all this work is firmly centred on the book, none of it is purely imitative, most of it is derivative in the widest sense. Nowhere does he ask his children simply to reproduce incident or character 'in their own words'. He either leads them directly and deeply inwards into the book itself (e.g. his section on Characters), or while using a particular part of the book as a jumping off point, he leads them outwards into all kinds of related experience.

The book was used as a basis for all English teaching for

four periods a week for ten weeks. His account of his teaching of it is as follows:

At the beginning of term the texts were handed out to the class and a short discussion was held on the programme of work with the novel for the term. They were asked to keep the book and read it in their spare time, and were also given opportunities to read it in class during silent reading periods. No attempt was made to read it round the class. Work based on the book began almost immediately and was usually initiated with a reading by me (the class following in their copies) of a selected passage. If the aim in that particular period was Creative Writing, a short discussion would follow, and then the class would be asked to write anything they pleased in prose or verse, suggested or inspired by the passage and our discussion. Later the writing was read out by the writers in turn and commented upon. Then the scripts were collected and read by me in depth, after which they were returned to the writers individually in a tutorial with my written comments.

If the aim was oral discussion, a theme suggested by the read passage was introduced by me and the subsequent discussion recorded on tape, which was later played back to the class. I found the tape-recorder an effective controlling medium leading to disciplined and relevant discussion. There was less disciplined discussion when for some reason the discussion was not recorded. Apart from introducing the theme and bringing the discussion back when it tended to flag or lapse into irrelevancy—hardly at all when it was taped—I allowed the discussion to range free and far outside the confines of the book to related experience in life. I shall give an example of this.

A short passage was read concerning the events leading up to the death of Maskew and a later passage concerning the events leading up to the death of the turnkey at Carisbrook Castle. In the first incident Elzevir Block was about to kill Maskew when Maskew was accidentally killed by the posse he has summoned to arrest the smugglers. In the second, Elzevir Block accidentally killed the turnkey while defending himself against the turnkey's murderous assault. The questions posed were: Would Elzevir have been justified in causing Maskew's death if the posse had not killed him? Was he in some way responsible for his death wounds? Was he justified in causing the turnkey's death? The discussion ranged far and wide and included a comparison between the penal laws of today and those of the eighteenth century (when smuggling was a capital offence); capital punishment; the right of private defence; the right or otherwise to kill in defence of property dishonestly acquired by oneself or a relative; the ethics of smuggling (*a*) small, (*b*) large, (*c*) expensive, (*d*) inexpensive articles through the Customs; the ethics of robbing the rich to give to the poor; is this all right as long as it is done by the Government? No particular attempt was made to reach a conclusion on any of the points raised. The discussion came to an end at the end of a period without a summing up. Another subject discussed on a separate occasion was the relationship between grown-ups and adolescents. This was triggered off by reading passages in which John Trenchard tells of his restricted life with his Aunt Jane and her treatment of him

For Impromptu Drama the class was divided into three groups. Dramatic situations were selected from the novel and given to the groups to improvise. They were asked to read the dialogue and description of the incident in the text, prepare a synopsis, then shut the book and improvise. They were advised to make no attempt to reproduce the original words, but to improvise their own words in modern English. Each group having improvised a different incident, they exchanged incidents, seeking to improve on each other's improvisations. Definite progress was noticeable.

The final stage in Drama was the improvisation of a class play with a modern setting, but suggested by a theme or situation in *Moonfleet*. After some discussion it was agreed that the story of *Moonfleet* could be summed up in several ways. Here are two examples:

'Unselfish and devoted friendship between two people brings them through great adversity until one dies in saving the other.'
'Violence begets violence and those that live by it may die by it.'

These in fact were the two themes chosen out of four for illustration by Creative Drama. The class individually each wrote a synopsis on one or other of these themes. The most promising were chosen for improvisation. The most successful was set in Eastern Europe and concerned a British spy condemned to confinement in a labour camp. He subsequently escapes and is recaptured, tried and sentenced to death. The

trial scene was recorded straight on to tape, as it was improvised, and was remarkably successful.

What impresses me most about this account of his subsequent
teaching of the book is that, because of his very careful and
thorough preparation of the book, the teacher knew exactly
where he was going with it and what he intended his children
to gain from it. At the same time it is clear from his account
that while the class benefited from his planning, he did not use
his prepared scheme as a 'blueprint' to be slavishly adhered to.
In any case it contained plenty of options and opportunities of
all kinds, but above all, his approach was flexible and his
scheme continually adapted to meet the needs of the class as
the book was read, discussed and dramatized.

Furthermore, although *Moonfleet* was quite consciously used
here as a structure upon which to base a whole term's work in
English and in this sense was a substitute for the use of a course
book, the work based upon it was very different from what the
conventional course book would have demanded.

The limited kind of language exercise which a course book
provides was avoided. Due attention was paid to the techniques
and mechanics of English usage, but always in a specific and
purposeful context. It was always the means to a more important end—never an end in itself.

THE SILVER SWORD

Ian Serraillier. (Heinemann—New Windmill Series—or Puffin
Books—Penguin)
Age-range: 11–14

While there is evidence of this book being successfully used
within the whole of the age-range mentioned above, the bare
figures are somewhat misleading in that most of the teachers
reporting on the book preferred to use it at eleven/twelve. My
own teaching experience would support this and I would
recommend this book as being generally very suitable for the
first two years of the secondary school, although there is a case
for its use later on with less able children.

There were varied reasons given for its particular success.

One teacher felt that it was a good book to begin literature teaching with as soon as children arrived in the secondary school, because it provided the right kind of shared experience for a class of eleven-year-olds and their teacher to get to know each other. Another noted that it was not easy to find a book which could be enjoyed by both boys and girls in an unstreamed class, but this was a book enjoyed, to a greater or lesser degree, by every child in the class.

Another reason for its success early on in the secondary school was produced by a number of teachers who felt that it was a good book for bridging the gap between purely children's books and more adult literature. While the book is easy for most children of this age to understand and to enjoy (there is an easy identification with the characters who are children, and their contacts with adults are brief and cursory) there is never any condescension towards the reader. Indeed, because of its subject ('It brings to life the current divisions of Europe and their causes and puts the eternal refugee problem in human terms') teachers found that it stretched the children and demanded comparatively mature thought.

It was reported to be a stimulus for the lethargic and the reluctant reader and encouraged some to use the library and read other books at home. At the same time several teachers felt that it was a very useful book for the backward. In writing of a mixed, less able class of thirteen-plus, it was recommended by one teacher because of its uncomplicated plot, simple but imaginative vocabulary, sympathetic characters and good story with the 'ring of authenticity'. Another teacher felt that the book was successful with the less able because of the physical and emotional difficulties which many such children have to face—the book provides the opportunity for helpful identification. Finally, the moral issues of war were dealt with sufficiently imaginatively for less able children to grasp them.

I think the last point is an important one, and the book is a small counterweight to the fictional picture of war presented to children on film and television and especially for those children most likely to be viewing this and least likely to be critical of it.

Treatment of the Book

A. Discussion

Usually the book was read aloud by the teacher with discussion taking place at relevant points. This was sometimes preceded by introductory lessons on the Second World War and work to clarify the geographical location of the story. Thus one teacher introduced the book as follows:

Before beginning the story the introduction was read and discussed. The time, setting and background of the story were then established. Reference was made to the geographical locations (with the aid of maps) of main cities and rivers mentioned in the book; the distance between Warsaw and Switzerland was also noted. A further lesson followed on the Second World War and its effects on Central Europe, especially those effects which have a direct bearing on the book, i.e. internment, work and prison camps, the breakdown of communication (roads, railways, etc.), the refugee problem and Swiss neutrality, etc.

The introduction of this kind of background material seems to me a useful contribution to the child's understanding of the book. But, as I have just noted in discussing *Moonfleet*, I feel there is a danger if it becomes too much of an end in itself. The literature teacher is chiefly concerned with the inter-relationship of character and the personal reactions of the children in the story to their problems—no other activities must be allowed to obscure this central concern too much. I am not suggesting that a knowledge of the historical background of the book is not important, or a geographical study of the journey related in the book of relevant interest, but I would suggest that perhaps these aspects of it could more effectively be tackled by the history and geography teacher. Where this is possible an integrated project with these particular colleagues might produce work of more value, not only to the literature teacher, but to the historian and geographer. The literature teacher is then free to restrict his discussion to the issues which arise from the personal experience of the book. Some of these discussions are pretty general and wide-ranging, but they all have obtained their initial impetus from a personal reaction to a personal situation.

Some discussion remained within the confines of the experience of the book and was chiefly concerned with the characters of the children in the story, their reactions to situations and the underlying motives for their actions.

e.g. Why did Jan attach himself to animals and objects?
Why did he steal?
How do their personalities change and develop?

Some discussion, on the other hand, moved outside the book, but still remained very personal:

e.g. Forgiveness.
Is it always wrong to steal? Would you steal to help your family? Should you always tell the truth? (i.e. Does the end justify the means?)

Again, at a personal, and one hopes chiefly imagined, level:

How would you feel if your own mother or father was taken away suddenly?
How do you think Joseph felt at being taken away?

Or more generally:

The problems of children parted from their parents by circumstances and the children having to accept adult responsibilities.
The problems of refugees. (What has happened to Second World War refugees now? The Red Cross, Refugee Camps, Organizations such as Oxfam, etc.)
Persecution—leading to racial discrimination. Fear. Cruelty —mental and physical.

A different kind of personal experience was drawn upon by the class which related Joseph's experience as a prisoner of the Nazis to what they had heard from their own fathers, uncles and acquaintances who had suffered in prisoner-of-war camps.

I do not feel that I have over-emphasized my concern for personal experience and a personal approach to the questions raised by this book with children of eleven/twelve. It seems to me that children of this age can only profitably consider such immense and complex topics as war or such abstract concepts as truth if they are presented to them in personal terms. Thus, of the various discussion topics listed and described in connection with *The Silver Sword*, perhaps the most appropriate was simply:

What is the effect of war on people?

B. Written Work

The written work on the book included:

The Book Review—Plot. Characters. Did you like it? Why? Was there any part you disliked? Why? Is it a book to recommend to other children?

I am never quite sure how useful such an assignment is at this age, except perhaps with an exceptionally intelligent class. It can too easily become a series of stock responses to a stock formula. I prefer the following:

The feelings of a prisoner on the night before an escape.
Newspaper accounts of Joseph's escape from different points of view.
'Could it happen here?' Individual and group short stories on refugees in England.
Compositions and poetry about refugee life—these were taped and discussed both from a literary and from an informative angle.
Poetry on themes arising from the book—'Fear', 'The Dark'.

All the above seem to me to be imaginative and relevant enough both to the experience of *The Silver Sword* and the children. One class, however, produced a summary of some scenes by means of leading questions and answers—the latter providing the summary. This is surely a misuse of the book and a complete misconception of the kind of written work which children of this age ought to be engaged in.

C. Drama

Improvisation
Improvisation (in groups) of incidents which the children had chosen.

e.g. Joseph Balicki's escape.
    Meeting with Jan.
    Episode with Bistro.
    Trial of Jan following the train robbery.
    Incident on Burgomaster Wollf's farm.
    Arrival in Switzerland.

Mime

e.g. The flight over the rooftops.
    The escaped monkey.

Group plays
Group scripted and unscripted plays on *similar* incidents to those in the book.

e.g. The problems of children who, through varying circumstances, are parted from their parents and who have to assume adult responsibilities.

Work emphasizing role-playing.

e.g. Ruth bringing up the family.

Work on more abstract concepts.

e.g. Fear.

Tape-recorded interviews on escape.

D. Language Work

It was pleasing to find that there were no examples worth noting of language work *per se* being undertaken in connection with the book. This was splendidly reassuring in that one would hope that, particularly with this kind of book and children of this age, most teachers would agree that any such activity would be misplaced.

The Case for Simply Reading
Despite the number of questionnaires received about *The Silver Sword*, the amount of information received about the book was comparatively slight. This is to be expected with younger classes. The options are fewer, the kind of discussion one can profitably hold more limited, written work is unlikely to include literary considerations and one is perhaps concerned,

45

above all else, with simple enjoyment. It therefore ought to be made quite clear that, as indeed is the case with all the other books individually discussed, the activities suggested are a synthesis of information received from a great many sources. Thus not only would it be undesirable to attempt too much in the way of related activities of whatever kind, but there is more positively a case for simply reading a book to children and leaving it at that.

A Hertfordshire teacher read *Kpo, the Leopard* with her class of twelve-year-old secondary modern girls for two periods a week for half a term:

The book was read to the class by me, while each child had a copy of the book in front of her. The only activity which accompanied the reading of the book was slight discussion as it arose naturally from the book. The class resented anything which actually stopped the reading of the book. They were utterly absorbed from the first word. They preferred any discussion to be over and finished with at the beginning of the lesson—based on what had been read in the previous lesson—and used really as a linking introduction into the next section. Any dramatic work or tape-recorder work was totally unnecessary, as the book was enjoyed completely as it should be, as a book.

A similar point-of-view was expressed by several other teachers in completing the questionnaire, and the view was by no means confined to the youngest or least able classes.

Other books which were specifically mentioned as successful with this kind of reading and which required very few other activities of any kind were:

John Masefield, *Jim Davis*
Gavin Maxwell, *Ring of Bright Water*
Alan Sillitoe, *The Loneliness of the Long-Distance Runner*
J. R. R. Tolkien, *The Lord of the Rings*

LORD OF THE FLIES
William Golding. (Faber or Penguin Books)
Age-range : 12–15

This book was successfully used in all kinds of school and with all kinds of class throughout a very wide age-range. However, despite the width of the age-range reported on (twelve/fifteen) most of the teachers using the book preferred to use it in the fourth or fifth year, and I would agree with them. I would think that to use it with a younger group, however well it is taught, would mean limiting the potential exploration of the very important issues which the book raises.

It was clearly the most popular of all the books reported on. Part of its popularity may be due to the current enthusiasm for it among the Examination Boards who evidently feel, almost as a corporate body, that at last they have discovered a book which is contemporary, relevant to the children and suitable for examination purposes. (There are other books which fulfil these criteria!) However, its use was reported in connection with five different 'O' level G.C.E. Boards; eight different external C.S.E. Boards and it was fairly frequently a Mode 3 C.S.E. choice on the part of individual teachers. It is a choice I would endorse, for, despite divided critical opinion as to its merits, both among the 'professionals' and among practising teachers, it is very evidently an outstandingly successful book for teaching purposes.

A teacher in a northern comprehensive school was interestingly explicit in his listing of the very varied reasons for his choice of the book:

This book is chosen for children emerging from childhood into adolescence for the following reasons:

(*a*) It provides a vehicle by means of which they can examine aspects of their own behaviour patterns by identification, thus removing their problems to the safe distance necessary for their contemplation without undue disturbance.
(*b*) It allows 'retreat into the story' if the realizations become too disturbing.
(*c*) It provides 'shock' treatment which helps speed the growing-up process.

The book is chosen for children emerging from childish into adult reading patterns for the following reasons:

(*a*) It affords examples of simplified character types which are easily comparable.

(*b*) It provides easy material for discussion of symbolism in literature.

(*c*) It provides material for discussion of the form of a book or the gradual development of a theme.

(*d*) It allows explanation of wh t is meant by climax.

(*e*) It affords examples of evocative descriptive passages.

(*f*) It affords an absorbing story which teaches that pleasure can be found in books which have a serious theme.

(*g*) It offers starting points for much work on themes involving further reading of prose and poetry.

Some, though not all, of these criteria were cited by many other teachers using the book. Many were more concerned with the social implications of the story than with some of the more literary criteria listed above. A secondary modern teacher who wrote 'it focused strong attention on the fragility of civilization and consequently implied a need to do something about preserving it' was making a point made by many others. A number of teachers also found this a particularly useful book for 'difficult' classes in that it stimulated discussion of such questions as law and order, authority and the individual. Another teacher noted: 'In discussing the book and society's need for laws, the interest of certain "troublesome" boys became actively engaged. They were very frank about their brushes with authority, in and out of school, and about their attitudes to authority. They became, more than usually, drawn into the class.'

Again, a comprehensive school teacher found the book relevant not only because of its particular place in her scheme of work (she had previously dealt with the theme of 'Crime and Punishment' and was moving on to 'War') but because she felt that the fourth year in a comprehensive school was disturbing and testing to all children, however well adjusted, and because 'in the class were two or three boys for whom problems of restraint, authority and anti-social urges were acute at the time'. In a simpler, and perhaps unfashionably old-fashioned sense, a secondary modern teacher noted simply: 'In a spirited and rather rebellious group of six to nine boys it produced some thoughtful and salutary recognition of the immaturity of boys and the towering stature—relatively—of an educated adult.'

Finally, in accounting for this book's success, one teacher not only summarized effectively what a great many others had said implicitly or explicitly, but also provided the complete and perhaps only justification for all our literature teaching:

The children grew up. They gained much in the understanding of life, other people and themselves. They were all involved in the book. It made a big impact and they were a good deal sobered, wiser and more tolerant for the experience. I think it *was* an experience. It also brought the teacher/class relationship much closer.

Treatment of the Book

A. Three Complete Approaches to *Lord of the Flies*

The first of these was with a mixed class aged fifteen-plus in a very large comprehensive school. The class was streamed in a very broad sense (each year in four broad streams) and the class concerned was in the B stream. The book was used outside the framework of any public examinations, for four periods a week for three weeks.

1. *The 'climate' of the class.* You must first understand that various tactics had been employed to suggest to the children that the success of a class was their responsibility—that the onus for their education was to be carried by them, as well as by me. We'd used different passages to discuss this idea (including, incidentally, a page or two from *The Disappearing Dais*).[1] The class regularly sat in a circle, and in discussion (on many occasions) I used to put my hand up if I wanted to contribute. The last speaker appointed the next (cf. Conch in *Lord of the Flies*) and at times I was cheerfully ignored!

2. The class read *Lord of the Flies* a couple of weeks before any discussion of it was held in class.

[1] F. Whitehead, *The Disappearing Dais*, Chatto and Windus, 1966.

3. On the first day of work on the book I had a note sent into the class, saying that I was delayed, but the class should start discussion on the book. I deliberately gave no more help than this. In fact, I was having a coffee in the staff room next-door-but-one, and could hear the bedlam: at first, that is. After fifteen to twenty minutes I went in, to find the class in perfect order (being run by a girl of very dominating personality). I issued paper and asked them to write a description of the last twenty minutes. Resentment here—'Why should we be punished—you shouldn't be late', etc.! After a while, the penny dropped—the opening chapter of *Lord of the Flies* had, in a sense, been *enacted* by the class. Interestingly enough, the class wanted to continue under Rose's chairmanship for the rest of the day! We discussed the papers, and the relevant first difficulties on the island, the next day.

4. Next, we split the class by sex (having talked about Golding's decision to have only one sex on the island). We then worked in two large groups. The class had to believe they were in the same position as the boys on the island—except *they* had read the book! How could they establish a pattern of life with built-in safeguards against the dangers which destroy the boys on the island? This discussion lasted (at great intensity) for three periods with each group. In general, the girls were more practical, the boys very theoretical. I took very little part here—simply sitting outside the circles (which were in different rooms—a teacher's *absence* seems very important to a group once it is really going well: no matter how I tried to be self-effacing, I felt I was an inhibiting factor). Very occasionally, I'd interject a question—usually in demand of a fuller explanation.

5. They then wrote a paper about the experience. I asked them to hypothesize on the future of their group. Which individual did they fear most in their group? (Several said 'Myself'!) Which character in the novel did they feel they themselves most closely resembled?

   (With another class, I tried starting off with a paper on similar lines with not nearly so successful results.)

6. Armed with these papers, we now turned to discussion of the individual characters. I had them work in four groups for a day—one group each for Simon, Jack, Ralph and Piggy. Each group then took the class in turn, introducing

their assessment of the character. Simon inevitably proved the most fascinating character. Once one suggested (and they did need the suggestion) an analogy to Christ—or at least a Martyr of the New Testament—they bit very eagerly. (Simon—Peter, man-on-the-hill, rejection of a Messiah, Gethsemane experience, etc.)

7. Inevitably wider issues occurred incidentally.
   e.g. Future of man.
        Nature of man—evil?
8. On a literary level, we considered the nature of allegory/ myth, the use of *Coral Island* (of which they'd never heard!), the need (or absence of need) for credibility in a literal sense, etc.
9. The book proved very useful as a yardstick in many later discussions, e.g. the problem of evil in *Macbeth*.

This approach to the book I felt to be of great interest. I am impressed by the obvious way in which, from the moment of the ingenious first lesson, the children were clearly very fully involved. It is also worth noting that in addition to the emphasis in this class on the individual responsibility of the pupil, and the large part played in its success by the contribution of the children, the teacher's role was a very vital one. As I have noted elsewhere, such a scheme was possible and successful because of careful and considered planning on the teacher's part, in this instance a combination of related discussion and written work which provided the pupils with a continual impetus.

The teacher concerned considers that such a teaching method could be applied to fourth or fifth forms and mentioned particularly C.S.E. classes and non-specialist English at 'A' level.

In the second example, the book was used in conjunction with G.C.E. and C.S.E. examinations, but both of the Mode 3 type; and the basis of the syllabus was wide reading rather than three or four 'set' books. The class was again a mixed one aged fifteen-plus and was the top stream out of four in a secondary modern school.

As someone has written in *The Use of English, Lord of the Flies* rarely fails to arouse strong feelings—among teachers and dons no less than among school and college students. I find the book a respectable piece of literature well worth reading, studying, pondering.

I am impressed by:

(a) The debunking of the *Coral Island* myth and the romantic *Robinson Crusoe*.

(b) Golding's highly relevant (to twentieth-century life) consideration of the effects of fear. Cf. also his *The Inheritors*.

(c) The implied importance in *Lord of the Flies* of adult knowledge and also artefacts in preserving a civilization.

(d) Political overtones—the importance in government of 'Good Men', clever men, naked force, democracy, visionaries.

An Oblique Approach

ASSIGNMENT 1. Read any hundred pages of *The Swiss Family Robinson* (a fairly typical example of the *Coral Island, Robinson Crusoe* genre). In fact nearly everyone read the whole book and said they liked it very much. They had one week-end for this task with a very strict time limit.

ASSIGNMENT 2. A test (on *The Swiss Family Robinson*) lasting for two (thirty-five minute) periods. Written work on such compulsory questions as:

(a) What artefacts were saved from the ship? (Artefact was well defined previously.)

(b) Briefly describe the beginnings of agriculture on the island.

(c) How were domesticated animals raised?

(d) Make a list of the engineering skills possessed by the father.

(e) What knowledge did the mother and father bring to the education of their young?

ASSIGNMENT 3. A far-ranging class discussion on civilization, its beginnings, the importance of traditional skills, language, education, the place of adults, the immaturity of children, the length of the learning process. This lasted for several periods.

ASSIGNMENT 4. Read Chapters I and II of *Lord of the Flies*. A strict time limit was enforced—forty-eight hours probably.

ASSIGNMENT 5. Written test.

(a) How did the boys come to be on the island?
(b) How does Golding 'get rid of' all adults?
(c) How does Golding 'get rid of' nearly all artefacts?
(d) What artefacts do the boys in fact possess?
(e) How old are the boys:
   (i) the oldest ones?
   (ii) Samaneric?
   (iii) the littluns?
(f) How do the boys behave during the first day?
(g) Very carefully describe the first appearance of Jack and the choir. Do their uniform and discipline suggest any modern political party?

The rest of our study followed the pattern of:

(a) Homework or class-reading of *Lord of the Flies*. For homework overnight reading was demanded or at most forty-eight hours was allowed.
(b) Discussion with the text in class, or
(c) Written test directing attention to what I think are the important 'strands' in the book. Then, following the written test, discussion of the answers.

Final thoughts. In class discussion, group discussion, pairs discussion and in written tests, we considered all the major 'strands' which I have listed and, in addition, the following:

  (i) How did *the fear* begin?
 (ii) Which leader, Jack or Ralph, offered the community the best chance of survival?
(iii) Who or what is Lord of the Flies? What is his idea of having fun?
(iv) Why did the boys lose much of their power of speech?

While this approach to the book may appear rather less exciting than our first example, I find it equally impressive. The teacher, by his use of *The Swiss Family Robinson*, also gives his children preliminary food for thought which enriches their subsequent reading of *Lord of the Flies* and greatly increases their understanding of it. His 'comprehension' questions aid and involve the children in this. Again I would like to emphasize the thorough preliminary thought and planning which ensured the success of this scheme.

The last full account of the teaching of *Lord of the Flies* is, I hope, of particular interest as it is concerned with a 'less able' group.[1] The class is from a large comprehensive school and consists of boys of fourteen-plus. It is the thirteenth stream down, out of thirteen streams.

I began the book with an open mind as to whether it would succeed. Only I had a copy and I read to the pupils, introducing the book only by saying that I wasn't sure whether they would like it, find it too difficult, etc. If so, they must tell me.

After two sessions of my reading it they said they would like to read the whole book and I got them copies. (Had it been apparent that it wouldn't go I should have used the part I had read as a springboard to some story writing, made a few links with mob behaviour which has cropped up in the school and left it at that.) However, the book was mechanically vastly difficult for them so we proceeded like this: I read most of it to them and they followed. (We discussed whether I should paraphrase difficult parts, but decided no—they tended to get lost when I diverged from the words on the page.) When a conspicuously easier passage was coming up, I would ask one of the abler readers to read the short passage. When the situation and people were fairly well established in their minds, exchanges of dialogue were read dramatically, i.e. between the appropriate number of voices. When I set a reading homework it was very short (five pages) and then only if I realized that a manageable section was coming up. The next lesson then began with the kind of talking about the section read at home, which would fill it in for those who'd failed, or not been able, to cope.

Written work. 'Death on the Island' (didn't have to be with reference to *Lord of the Flies*) at the point when violence to humans was obviously imminent, but hadn't happened.

Which would you rather be—Jack or Ralph? Why? (This produced some surprisingly perceptive insights into what made the two boys in the story tick and what motives govern the pupils' own conduct.)

[1] For further accounts of work with 'less able' children, please see page 72.

A group of stories (some fiction, some not) on group be-
haviour, intervention of authority, etc., from beginnings such as :
'I knew they were waiting for me.'
'I ran towards the noise.'
'Looking back it's hard to understand.'

After thus describing the work on the book, the teacher
went on to comment as follows : 'The class was potentially a
very difficult one whose standard of involvement and attention
while working on this book was very high. The day we were
finishing it they all voluntarily stayed on into the dinner hour
to do so ! When we were reading the killing of Simon a spontaneous chant of "Kill the Pig" arose.'

In considering the success of the book with these children,
the teacher again commented on the high level of involvement
of the children.

They concentrated so keenly on the reading, their language
power must have developed. They wrote eagerly and quite
successfully whereas many would often be reluctant to put
pen to paper and certainly to produce homework. It provided
a framework for discussion of behaviour within their own
situation (and the kind of behaviour by which a lower ability
group often feels it necessary to assert itself) because the con-
flicts of the book are so accurately those of their own lives. (It's
conspicuous that they completely reject the actual ages of
Ralph, etc. Their assumption that the children are about their
own age or only a year younger, i.e. 'like us, but not so
sensible'! is more or less unshakeable.)

In the case of this group the fact that they were coping with
an expressedly difficult book gave them a sense of achievement.

If we think about the three complete schemes of work just
described, it will be apparent that each of the teachers concerned felt that the way in which the children were led into the
book was of unusual importance and influenced its subsequent success. We have thus already noted three differing
methods : an attempt to reproduce a state of anarchy in the
classroom out of which experience a really meaningful discussion could evolve; a preliminary and contrasting consideration of *The Swiss Family Robinson* (other classes read *Coral*

Island and *The Kon-Tiki Expedition* in exactly the same kind of way and for the same reasons); finally a teacher with a less able class who was anxious to interest and involve the children in the book, and who was able to arouse this interest without 'foisting' the book upon unwilling recipients.

Most teachers of intelligent children favoured a fairly gentle and perhaps more traditional approach. A typical scheme begins with a preparatory discussion of 'Power'. ('How do you get it? Use it? How could it be used? Who has real power today in the family, school, friends, nation? What are the dangers of power?') The beginning of the book is read in class to provide practice in reading aloud, practice in listening, vocabulary work and as a stimulus to further discussion. The rest of the book is then read at home. Alternatively the book is read by the pupils before any work begins upon it. Then a chapter, sometimes two, is taken week by week and the development of the book's themes discussed in detail. The story is taken for granted and each lesson centres around a few passages which are read in detail.

Such methods are familiar to and are used successfully by many teachers of our brighter children. However, the success of this book with the average and below average child is very marked. A teacher describing his work with a non-academic (C.S.E.) class in the East End of London wrote as follows:

The problem with teaching less academic pupils is to make abstract concepts (like 'responsibility' or 'primitive savagery') come alive for them, and whatever your approach you are ultimately at the mercy of your material. I found *Lord of the Flies* excellent material in this respect. The pupils responded well to every lesson, and took the work seriously. The connection between abstract concepts and the concrete material in the book was easily made, and the allegorical level of meaning, once pointed out, was explored with a minimum of direct teaching. The quality of oral response was much higher with this book than with others studied, and written work correspondingly better. One or two pupils previously unresponsive produced work of unprecedented quality. Many kinds of work are possible with this book, and I found it admirable for each of the kinds I tried, without any sense of having exhausted its potential.

I would endorse this teacher's concern for the right kind of material, for the less and for the more academic child. Yet while agreeing that in one sense a teacher is at the mercy of his material, I wonder if he doesn't perhaps under-emphasize the importance of the appropriate approach to it.

B. Discussion

No other book reported upon raised such a wide-ranging and varied number of issues for discussion. Some of these were specifically related to the book and perhaps differed little from the kind of written work that might be expected of more able children. A minority were concerned with purely literary issues.

e.g. (a) Does the degeneration build up logically or is it suddenly imposed?
  (b) How is the threat of violence suggested even in earlier scenes?
  (c) How long does the story take from beginning to end? Is it likely that it could happen all in this time?

However, the book is one which, of its own nature, enforces consideration of issues which are not literary in the narrow sense. It is noticeable that those teachers who begin with a discussion too narrowly rooted in the book find themselves almost immediately having to move outside it.

e.g. Was it lack of positive leadership from Ralph that made the other boys go over to Jack, rather than Jack's forcefulness? ('Here I tried to raise the question of certain political leaders, e.g. Hitler, but the class found this difficult to follow.')
or The characters and their interaction. ('This fairly rapidly became a discussion related to situations and clashes in school life, with other comments drawn from the children's experience of people and events.')
or How did the novel differ from the kind of story one would expect to read about young boy castaways on a desert island? (Comparison again with *Coral Island* and Graham Greene's *The Destructors*.)

Discussion based upon the book but more consciously moving rapidly outside it included such topics as : How do you

57

imagine you yourself would react in a similar situation? Analogies with the school structure often led to a discussion of law and order in the school context.

e.g. School Rules—Are all rules necessary? Who should make them? How are they enforced? Are any punishments just? How could the rules be improved?

Some pupils clearly sat on the other side of the school's disciplinary fence and also gained something from this kind of discussion. One teacher commented, 'Many of the form are prefects, house-captains, etc., and they relate Ralph's position as a chosen leader to their own. It has dawned upon them (especially the girls) that leadership may bring with it more pain than pleasure.' One class wondered if public schoolboys would be even more susceptible because of excessive regimentation. Chapter Ten was not only related to tyranny, full-scale war and its attendant horrors, but also to fights in the playground.

The book also provided opportunities for a more general discussion of adolescent behaviour outside as well as inside the school.

e.g. Would there have been any difference had girls and not boys been marooned on the island? The problems raised by the youth of the children and the lack of adults—do boys only behave themselves when adults are around? Are schoolboys more likely to become savages in these circumstances because they are used to obeying adults' orders unquestioned? Which are the laws which prohibit young people from doing things that adults are free to do? Why were such laws made? Should they be changed? How would you alter them?

Other classes moved well beyond the problems of mere adolescence to consider such basic and Socratic questions as:

The nature of man—what can be expected of him in his present stage of development?
The meaning of civilization—skin deep or not?
The nature of government—democracy and individual responsibility—totalitarianism and the rights of the individual.

Others again considered such abstract topics as trust, loneliness, fear and mass hysteria. A discussion of Simon in one
instance led on to mysticism (linked with T. S. Eliot's *Four
Quartets*), passivity, meditation ('flower-people'), ghosts,
U.F.O.s, the 'beast'. More socially or politically minded classes
concerned themselves with the 'power game', personality
cults, censorship and more specifically with the effect of environment and upbringing upon the personality or with
priorities in organizing a primitive society.

One particular class, which clearly had gained a great deal
from the book, covered much of the ground already mentioned by considering the following polar concepts in connection with their reading of it.

> Personal relationships / Social responsibility
> Intelligence / Brute force
> Culture / Savagery
> Mind / Emotion
> Activity / Passivity
> Primitive and not so primitive religion.

Clearly then, another reason for this book's popularity and
success is that directly or indirectly it poses so many questions
which can lead to a very worthwhile discussion at very different levels. With younger or less able classes it is possible to
do this in a very immediate way by considering the book in
relation to the immediate school situation; with more able or
more mature classes it raises questions basic to our whole
civilization and experience of life in the broadest and deepest
sense.

C. Written Work

Perhaps because this book, as we have just seen, lends itself
so well to discussion of all kinds at all levels, and also, as we
shall see, to Drama, the range and scope of written work
undertaken in connection with it seemed comparatively disappointing. Many of the topics set, understandably enough in
classes which were preparing for examinations, were very
much of the traditional 'O' level kind.

e.g. Describe the character of Piggy as it is brought out in his relations with Ralph and Jack.

or   Trace the stages by which Ralph lost his authority over the others. Give your opinion as to why Jack was able to take his place as leader.

Some were more general and involved the larger issues, but were still concocted very much with an eye on the examiners.

e.g. When he wrote *Lord of the Flies*, William Golding was thinking about the presence of good and evil, civilization and savagery, side by side in the same world. Discuss this statement.

or   'The influence of adults on children'—is this a true description of the theme of the book?

The ability to answer such questions adequately is a prerequisite of the examination system, but there would surely be far more of value to the pupil in the kind of penetrating 'comprehension' questions already described on page 53 or the kind of written work arising directly from real or imagined personal experience described (with very different children) in two of the three accounts of complete approaches to the book.

The following questions, immediately related to the child in a personal sense, seem to me to be far more worth the effort of a written answer, even by our intelligent fifteen/sixteen-year-olds.

If your form were cast away on the island, what would be the problems?

If I were Jack . . .

How would I feel if I were Simon . . .

Describe a scene in which you watch someone breaking a law which many people consider to be of little importance. At the end of Chapter Ten (Piggy's glasses have finally been stolen) the children were asked: 'You have been washed up alone on the boys' island at this point. How would you set about restoring order?' (To be written either as a story continuation or in the form 'I would . . .')

D. Drama

I have earlier discussed the way in which a great many teachers felt that the way this book was approached was particularly important. One of the most effective approaches I came across used Drama as a lead in to the book. I was present at the lesson described and it was certainly one of the most exciting 'literature' lessons I was privileged to witness.

The lesson took place in an Army Cadet hut, some distance from the main buildings of a secondary modern school in the West of England. The surroundings were drab and somewhat uninviting, but there was more space than could be obtained in the ordinary classroom and the place had the tremendous advantage that any accompanying noise did not disturb others. The lesson was taken by a Drama specialist, who also teaches some English. It must be emphasized that this was not an ordinary lesson, but a demonstration by the teacher of how he would use Drama to lead in to the book with a fourth-year class. It therefore contains more material than one ordinary lesson would. The teacher described his intentions as follows:

AN INTRODUCTORY LESSON TO 'LORD OF THE FLIES'

PRELIMINARY NOTES

It contains far too much unrelieved intensity of feeling and ordinarily I would spread it over several lessons.

These children know little or nothing about the book and the purpose of the lesson is to whet their appetites to read it and to study it in detail later on.

I shall try to create an atmosphere which will nourish a variety of moods.

Moods will change quickly: happy and carefree, fear of the unknown which lurks in the darkness and at the top of the mountain, the feeling of distaste for the knife and the blood which is only made bearable by the frenzied excitement of the hunt. Simon's climb up the mountain will go through fear of the unknown beast and the determination to find out the truth and rationalize, nausea at the sight of the dead man, compassion for him as a human being, relief that the beast does not exist and happiness that his quest has proved him right.

THE LESSON

1. Introductory exercise to relax in the heat of the sun turning to agony and fear. (Commentary and music from tape made by teacher.)
2. Carefree walk through uninhabited coral island. (Music 'Morning' from Grieg's *Peer Gynt* suite.)
3. Fear as night comes on, black night, shapes loom up and a strange fear takes hold of you, a feeling of the unknown. (Teacher began to talk of the 'beast' here. Music *Octandre* by Varèse.)
4. Children divide into groups of five or six. Choose a leader —Jack. Organize a pig hunt. Track the animals through the undergrowth—sharpened sticks for weapons. You find pigs asleep in a clearing. Jack points out the victim and you all pounce with your spears. You have never killed before and you can't bring yourself to do it unless you shout, dance and scream. Feelings of dislike return when Jack cuts off the head and sticks it on a spear stuck in the ground as a gift for the beast. Fall silent when you think of the beast. Begin in silence. End in silence.
5. Spread out. You are Simon. You do not really believe in the beast. You decide to find out. [Teacher gives the following running commentary during this exercise.]

'You decide to investigate and climb the mountain to see. You feel rather unhappy about it, but you make yourself go on. As you near the top of the mountain you go slowly and crouch down, taking cover from trees, bushes and rocks. Then you see it. You stop dead in your tracks. For a moment you freeze with horror. But wait! What is it? If only the sun was not so strong. Cautiously you go nearer and you can see with relief what it is. It's a dead airman hanging on a parachute entangled in the trees.

'Your feelings change from fear to disgust. The man has been dead some time and the look and the smell are horrible. Look at the poor ruined face and begin to feel sorry for this poor human being. Who was he? Where did he live? Whose father was he? Whose husband? Whose son?

'So with pity you cut the cords which hold him up to the indignity of the wind and the flies. He sinks into the undergrowth and is covered with the green ferns. Your feelings change again as you realize that there is no beast, you are happy to know that you were right. You must tell the others.'

[The teacher was very successful in building up an atmosphere of fear and foreboding and at the end a contrasting feeling of great relief.]

6. Wild uninhibited modern dance deliberately introduced to wipe out the horror.

I also observed the same teacher teach another lesson with a different group. This consisted of two short scenes from the book which the class had been previously working upon. The children acted their own versions of these episodes which were:

1. Samaneric at the signal fire see the 'beast'.
2. The conflict between Ralph and Jack about the priority of hunting or the signal fire.

The latter was particularly effective. The teacher explained that he had tried to realize the conflict of will between Ralph and Jack. The scene was superbly controlled and the conflict and interplay of character very strong.

These children were clearly getting the experience and 'feel' of the book in a way which it would be difficult to achieve by any other method. I am convinced that these skills ought to be part of the basic professional equipment of all teachers of literature and that the present system of teacher training ought to take more account of this. I am equally convinced that this teacher's effectiveness as a Drama teacher is partly based upon his skill and knowledge as a teacher of literature, also. The view that Drama should be fused with English teaching in schools is one that some Drama specialists strongly oppose. I am more than ever convinced after meeting this particular teacher that drama and literature teaching are the more effective if the same teacher has responsibility for both.

There may be teachers who feel that they lack the knowledge or experience to attempt the kind of work just described. (They might well surprise themselves and their children if they tried it!) Dramatic reading is not Drama in the same sense, but, as previously suggested, it can bring the book effectively to life and does not require the comparatively soundproof space which is often not available. A comprehensive school teacher made effective use of this method of reading in tackling *Lord of the Flies.*

We read it straight through in class and often individuals in the class took a character so as to dramatize the effect. It was remarkable sometimes how involved otherwise dull readers became, so that they managed this without mistaking who said what, as sometimes happens with this method. Occasionally someone read straight passages of description, etc., apart from me, but this is always less successful so we had that infrequently. . . . I would interrupt the reading frequently to ask questions, to illuminate the meaning or remind us of what had gone before, or bring out someone's character, or point to some interesting aspect of the drama of it—to show the novel's complexity. Occasionally this would break into discussion. . . . The class were all thinking hard about it and needed only to probe a bit further to get them thinking more deeply still.

E. Language Work

There was little specific mention of language work in connection with this book—presumably most teachers and classes were too deeply entrenched in the philosophical problems it raised! There was mention of vocabulary work arising from reading aloud in class and one teacher found that the quality of the descriptive writing in the book was such that it led to the kind of analysis and discussion usually only possible from poetry.

SHORT STORIES OF OUR TIME
Edited by D. R. Barnes. (Modern English Series. Harrap)
Age-range: 13–15 (the age-range within which the book was normally used is not as wide as these figures suggest. Although I had one example of the book being used well with thirteen-year-old children, all the other teachers reporting on the book preferred to use it in the fourth or fifth year)

This book was used with great success in grammar and independent schools and in the top streams of comprehensive schools. On the evidence I have, it was not used very much in secondary modern schools, although, as we shall see later, there was an interesting example of its use in a secondary modern school.

The book succeeded primarily because it contains a well-balanced selection of stories which interest both boys and girls. It is, furthermore, a book which can be appreciated at all levels. As one grammar school teacher put it, rather bluntly perhaps: 'The dimmer ones can pass an exam question on it and the brighter ones can take it much further. In a mixed ability group, there is the chance of everyone being involved.' (I find its apparent non-use by secondary modern schools puzzling. The stories in the book are easy to follow, and if they were read to slower readers I would expect them to get quite a lot from them, for reasons I am about to discuss.)

One teacher felt that not only is the material in the book well varied, but the contents are well suited to an age at which children are ready to become involved in more difficult literature, are beginning to move into analytical and conceptual talk, and begin to examine and evaluate relationships and emotional experiences in public terms. The book succeeds in meeting these needs at exactly the right level. 'It sparked off discussion of topics relevant to their own experiences, or merely said something to them about their own experience. It often added something to what we had already been discussing . . . [it] gives them an enlarged understanding of their own and other people's problems'—this observation was echoed by all the teachers reporting on the book.

Thus the book succeeds largely because it is a good selection of stories, closely related to life and to the growing child's experience of life. From the teacher's point of view it is also successful because each story readily provides a starting-point for discussion, and the relationship between the stories is such that in whatever order they are read, or whatever other material is used in conjunction with them, a common element can readily be found. Further, the stories allowed many of the most basic questions about human life to be considered closely, e.g. loneliness, mass justice, over-protective parents, the effect of public concern, the frustration felt with the older generation. The book thus lent itself particularly well to topic or thematic treatment.[1] One teacher noted that it could be linked very effectively with the extracts in *Reflections* and with articles of social concern appearing in the *Guardian*. ('We spent four weeks on old people as a result of reading *Uncle Ernest*.')

There was some disagreement about the 'literary' value of the book. One teacher, who was using the book most effectively in other ways and for other reasons, did not want to use the stories as examples of good writing as she did not feel that the stories would stand up to close criticism. However, others felt that the stories lent themselves well to the discussion of short-story technique and different styles of writing. 'It introduces them to a range of styles in the writing, most of which are within their comprehension and some of which are later reflected in their own work.' Another teacher found the book useful for some kinds of 'language' work. 'The standard of writing is such that close study is profitable, e.g. *Through the Tunnel* can be analysed in groups as an introduction to Précis.'

Some teachers considered that when their children reached the fourth and fifth year most of their reading of novels ought to be organized on an individual basis. However, they still felt the need for common material so that discussion was based upon a common experience and answers formulated from common ground. The short story was particularly useful for this. Finally, it was felt that the short story was an effective means of introducing a child to an author and that the children were often led through the short story to other more major works of literature by the same author.

Treatment of the Book

A. A Thematic Approach

I am grateful to a teacher in the Midlands for allowing me to reproduce the account of her teaching of the book which follows. The book was used in a city grammar school in a very deprived area. It was an 'O' level set text (Cambridge Board). The class was an unstreamed mixed ability group. The book

[1] See page 11 for specific list of what this book may have achieved with one class.

was used for fifteen lessons over a period of twenty weeks (plus homework time). Sometimes two or three lessons were taken on it together; sometimes the book was left for a week or so. The book was read partly in class and partly at other times.

The stories could be grouped into themes—some stories falling into more than one group, of course. Thus we could discuss contemporary problems such as: 'Growing up'; 'Relationships between children and parents'; 'Problems of old people'; 'Justice'; 'Crime and punishment'; 'Death and our attitudes to it'; 'News reporting'; 'Effects of gossip and mass opinion'.

Sometimes these discussions arose out of the story; sometimes independent discussion on such topics would lead us naturally into one of the stories in a later lesson. Often debates, poetry, drama and these short stories would link together in one big 'barney' lasting for a week or more on a problem of real concern to the children. (Before continuing, may I point out the danger of the 'questions for discussion' at the end of the book. Despite the warnings that these were for discussion only, the children seem to expect written work based on these as exams loom nearer; and they are tempting for an 'easy' lesson.)

Some topics I conducted are as follows:

A. *Newspapers*. We had compared various newspaper accounts of Donald Campbell's death during this year. This easily led on to discussion of 'distortion' by newspaper men and public opinion. We read *Shot Actress—Full Story* in the light of this discussion. An essay was written at home on the same topic. Also work was done individually on distortion of facts by various newspapers.

B. *Justice, or Crime and punishment*. We read *Late Night on Watling Street*. First I just let them enjoy this story. Most were just fascinated by how the man could kill the police. Then we led on (in a later lesson) to a discussion of who was in the wrong? Should someone have reported the action? Was Jackson sufficiently punished? This led on to a discussion (vague!) about the meaning of justice. There was an easy link from here to *Dry Rock*. What here was the principle? Justice? Whose was the greatest fault? We spent one lesson comparing Tarloff in *Dry Rock* with Shylock (*The Merchant of Venice* was also set for

'O' level this year). The children themselves saw this link, and a violent discussion ensued. As a result we staged an independent mock trial of an 'underdog'.

C. *Problems of old people.* Stories like *Life of Ma Parker, Present for a Good Girl, Uncle Ernest* were used here. We linked them to their own experience by considering problems of their own aged relatives: poverty, loneliness, lack of understanding. We looked at pensions tables, surveyed local old people's homes, etc. Specific questions were asked in relation to the old people considered in the story.

D. *Growing up and understanding between parents and children.* First we read *A Message from the Pigman*. This quickly leads into the question of why children are afraid of asking parents questions and why misunderstandings grow up. We particularly considered why children are unable to ask parents about sex. This fear of questions was compared with the boy Ekky in the story. Gross misunderstanding by parents of their child came out in *Little Pet*. The way children grow up through various experiences was explored in *Through the Tunnel* and *The Living*.

Written Work

When I visited this teacher, she was able to give me a detailed account of the written work which had been done. This was consciously divided into non-exam-based and exam-based work:

1. *Non-exam-based work*

(*a*) We researched into the situations as they are locally. (Old people—where do they live? In homes, with their families or on their own?) We looked into pensions and supplementary pensions. (Do the old people get as much as they need?) This was related to the stories *Uncle Ernest* and *Present for a Good Girl*.

(*b*) We looked at the lonely and the outcast in society—dealing with Jews, coloured people, old people, children (mother's boys, and orphans). We used some records here—'I Am a Rock', 'They're Coming to Take Me Away, Ha, Ha', some Bob Dylan and Joan Baez; also poems, e.g. Auden's 'Say This City'. The unavailability of jobs was discussed. Relevant *Guardian* articles were used. The film *To Sir with Love* was seen by some of the class and discussed.

(*c*) We wrote imaginative stories under the titles of 'The Out-sider' and 'Conversation between Neighbours' (about some-body who is going to move into the street). This kind of thing is applicable here as there are a number of Poles in the area and many Jewish children in the school. We also did a con-versation between a mother and her daughter as to why the daughter should or should not go out with a coloured man. This can take discussion a lot further. The children could show their prejudice without actually admitting that they were by putting their thoughts into the mouths of neighbours.

2. *Exam-based work*
(*a*) We answered some of the questions at the back of the book in rough and used these as a basis for discussions. I some-times modified the questions and sometimes made up my own.
(*b*) They would read a story in class and we would use it as a basis for discussion in the next lesson, or they read as a home-work task and then we would discuss in class.
(*c*) Written work.
   (i) Tell the events of the story briefly and draw some con-clusions.
   (ii) What have you learned about old people?
   (iii) Comparison between two stories—*Dry Rock* can be used side by side with *Late Night on Watling Street*.
   (iv) Questions on 'justice'. Should they have been brought to justice? Whose fault was it that they weren't? (*Late Night on Watling Street*). This was linked with Shylock from *The Merchant of Venice*.
   (v) Children and the process of growing up.
   (vi) Relationship of children with parents. *Little Pet* and *A Message from the Pigman* were used for this, the task being to discuss the relationship between each boy and his parents. In what way are they similar and how do they differ?

The most striking thing about this teacher's work with the book is the way in which she has refused to capitulate to the demands of the examiners or to 'play safe' with the book from the examination point of view. She concentrated chiefly on what she felt was educationally right and desirable for the class and gradually led, in her written work, from a subjective and personal consideration of the stories to an ability to answer a question specifically and more objectively than before. Incidentally, her examination results were good.

B. Three Other 'Discussion' Approaches to the Book

1. Another teacher I visited was teaching the book to a fifth form (top stream out of two) in a girls' secondary modern school.

She also found that every story provided a basis for very worthwhile discussion which she called 'Points of Departure'. Here are two examples, from the two stories in the book I have not so far referred to:

Possessions
The clinging to a past, symbolized in material objects. The linking of characters who, though unlikely to come together, find common longings or those which can be readily understood by the other character. The transitory character of some hopes as they are replaced by others.

The Raid
A good example of a story, the interpretation of which varies as it progresses. An understanding of fear and how it manifests itself in different characters—room to manœuvre your thoughts in the eventual outcome. An excellent opening to create atmosphere and an explanation at the end. With brighter children an identification of elements in the story with elements in the inherited material of life, e.g. Christianity.

Written Work

In addition to the kind of far-ranging and fairly complex discussion, just described, this teacher found that the book lent itself to several different kinds of written work.

e.g. 'Literary' criticism—usually arising from the child's own choice of a story.
Parallel stories written by the children, sometimes reflecting some of the characters in the stories in the book.
The statement of opinion, e.g. Do principles matter? (*The Dry Rock*). Thematic work, e.g. loneliness—using several stories from the book in connection with the following poems: 'The Bull', Ralph Hodgson (*Poems of Spirit and*

Action). 'Miss Thompson Goes Shopping', Martin Armstrong (*Fresh Fields*). 'First Flight', Vernon Scannell (*Here Today*).

Creative writing—using a passage from a story, or a complete story, or the idea in a story, as a stimulus.

2. *Mixed Quaker independent boarding school 15+ unstreamed G.C.E. 'O' level class*

The method we mostly used was to appoint two pupils to prepare a spoken introduction to the story to be given at the start of the lesson. They could collaborate and produce one introduction or consult and produce a separate introduction each. We sometimes paired pupils who were known to have very differing views of the value of a story.

The introductions were usually five to ten minutes long, after which we naturally felt [our way towards] general discussion with either me or the introducer acting [as] chairman. Out of the discussion the pupils wrote their own notes, being both a general record of what was said and the pupil's own reflections or reservations upon it.

3. *London comprehensive school 13+ mixed class. Top stream of nine streams. A group approach*
(*a*) *Late Night on Watling Street* read to the class.
(*b*) Defined and discussed ideas of Theme and Realization in reference to their writing.
(*c*) Drew out, then developed ideas about themes of *Late Night on Watling Street*, and talked about problems and decisions of characters.
(*d*) The children selected a story from the book, then were grouped according to their selection. Read, discussed and wrote in groups on these questions:
  (i) What kind of experience is the story about?
  (ii) Have you ever met or known of a similar experience in life or fiction?
  (iii) How is the experience given life and actuality in the story?
Follow-up work—Write on theme of your own choice.
Teacher's role—To work with groups or individuals—discussion on major issues (death, loneliness), teasing out meaning (questions on significant detail from both teacher and pupils), personal relevance, language problems (How can I explain . . .? etc.).

71

Chapter Four

THE LESS ABLE

All pupils, including those of very limited attainments, need the civilizing experience of contact with great literature, and can respond to its universality, although they will depend heavily on the skill of the teacher as an interpreter. . . . In so difficult a task the teacher will need a greatly extended range of books from which to choose. . . .

Half Our Future.[1] Para. 473

We are here concerned with a very large number of children in the middle group of each (secondary modern) age-range. They fall midway between, on the one hand, those who can be defined as 'remedial', and, on the other hand, those whose abilities and attainments put them in the top third of the secondary modern school and thus ensure for them a fairly successful and clear-cut career leading to C.S.E. Certainly they form a sizeable percentage of the intake of any secondary modern (or comprehensive) school and they are very often neglected as a consequence of our concern for their more, or less, gifted brothers and sisters.

The syllabus of the Practical Studies Department of a Hertfordshire mixed secondary modern school is aimed specifically at this group. This syllabus stresses the integration of subject material and the development of the individual child, putting the child very much at the centre. When discussing the children, it goes on to say that 'The children who fall within the range of this department tend to be under-privileged, socially, culturally, linguistically, and generally, in terms of a lack of opportunities for living a full, rich, life. In teaching these children, we must attempt to make good the deficiencies

[1] *Half Our Future. A Report of the Central Advisory Council for Education (England).* H.M.S.O. 1963.

by providing the basis for a full rich life.' It goes on to emphasize their inarticulacy—'Language is the barrier. We must make them articulate by providing conditions which will enable them to converse, think, discuss, argue and make decisions. Reading and Writing follow after.' The syllabus goes on to discuss briefly the isolation of these children, their difficulty in developing personal relationships with others and how in a practical sense they can be helped and given independence and responsibility.

If most of us dislike what we regard as the arbitrary distinction between English Language and English Literature, we must now ask ourselves, when considering these children, whether the labelling of any activity as English and as having a peculiarly 'English' end is not equally misleading. At the same time, as my quotation from the Newsom Report is intended to emphasize, we must not lose sight of what literature can uniquely offer them.

Finally, as the Hertfordshire syllabus puts it: 'Practical Studies means Action rather than words, or doing things instead of writing essays about doing things.' It would be a truism to say that all the teachers who have contributed to this Report are concerned with the *active* participation and involvement of their pupils. However, with less able children most especially it must be a fundamental principle. The 'English' skills which are our particular concern, will not follow otherwise.

RUSH TO JUDGEMENT
Mark Lane. (Penguin Books)
used in conjunction with the Jackdaw Special Folder THE ASSASSINATION OF PRESIDENT KENNEDY (Jonathan Cape)
Age-range 14–15 (less able children—probably best read in the third term in the fourth year or in the first two terms of the fifth year)

This book was used with outstanding success within the age and ability range indicated above.

Its appeal lies in the fact that it reads almost like a fictional work, it is concerned with a great murder mystery and is almost a super epic in the best Hollywood tradition. However, unlike the film epic, the book is concerned with the truth of a real situation and part of its success is directly due to this fact. It is about a great historical event which took place within the lifetime of the children reading the book and which they remember clearly.

The book's value from the teacher's standpoint is that it contains no set answers; it is an open-ended book designed to make the reader think. The chief aim of the teacher using the book was 'to push back frontiers' and 'open up new ideas' and to force the children to realize that they themselves mustn't hold a preconceived view. 'I wanted to cast doubts on Mark Lane and the Warren Report. I want them to realize that in a democracy everyone has to make a decision. We mustn't rely on our Governments being right all the time—a personal stand and a personal decision. A perfect example of how human judgement can err—I wanted them to experience and be involved in—why did Kennedy die ?'

At the same time (and no doubt this contributed towards his success with the book) this teacher revealed an exceptional and heartening social and political concern: 'I attempt to show what my attitudes are, if I'm conscious of them and they (the children) are, some good must come out of stuff so involved in social questions. This is surely better than non-commitment, non-involvement. Other teachers have other views. If we aren't committed in this way, I don't see what education is all about.'

This teacher felt that, with this particular kind of child, a large measure of what they did must be oral work (shared experience again). 'I attempt to get them to discuss and argue. I want them to sort out what they believe themselves. Occasionally I go right out on a limb to do this. They have a background of me putting myself up as a sitting duck.'

He was very concerned that his children should realize that it was normal for adults to enjoy books of this sort and aware of the dangers of devising activities for his children which 'can get too gimmicky'. 'Newsom children must not be sold short—they must have stuff in full measure.' Another advantage of *Rush to Judgement* is that, despite its formidable length, the children could start anywhere. It is possible to take any starting point, e.g. Chapter Four, 'The Magic Bullet', and by getting a group of children really involved in one particular aspect of the story to work outwards from this point to involve them in a great deal more.

Treatment of the Book

I am most grateful to a Hertfordshire teacher for allowing me to reproduce the following account of his teaching of the book to a fifth-year mixed secondary modern class. It was the bottom stream of three and the book was used for four periods a week over three weeks as part of a C.S.E. course.

1. I outlined the accepted facts of the assassination of Kennedy, leading up to the Warren Commission and Mark Lane's book.
2. I gave a brief history of Kennedy—his career and personal life, and his image as the President.
3. I took a number of points and gave the Commission's view and Lane's queries:

   Where the shots came from (page 11)
   The magic bullet (page 47)
   Why Oswald was wanted (page 60)
   The murder of Officer Tippit (page 162)

   The class were then asked to browse through the book and the Jackdaw Special Folder and to discuss any point with me or with classmates.

After two lessons of browsing, the class were asked to select any aspect of the assassination (as indicated in the chapter headings of the book) and to write illustrated essays, making it quite clear which were accepted and undisputed facts, which were the Warren Commission's findings—based on the investigations of the Police, F.B.I. or whatever—which were from Mark Lane's book, and which were their own ideas.

I obtained other books about Kennedy, including the summary of the Warren Commission's Report, and these were available for reference.

The topic and the literature evoked a terrific response and interest, and the individual studying done by all pupils was of a relatively high standard. Concentration was excellent, and the oral work was of a very high standard.

The main 'work' or results were:

1. Oral work—discussion and argument.
2. Summaries.
3. Their own views and opinions based on the evidence and ideas they could obtain.

I tried hard initially to 'attack' the official Warren Commission's Report, then I switched to putting all my weight behind the Warren Commission, since stimulation was essential in order to rouse the class.

I likened the assassination to the greatest murder mystery in the history of the world, with clues, suspects, motives and results (Tippit and Ruby and Oswald—all dying) all available.

I referred too to *Daughter of Time* (Josephine Tey), read also that year, and to the need for moderate dissatisfaction and questioning of everything done in our name—the essence of democracy and the antithesis of totalitarianism.

The final all-important question, 'Does it really matter who did what?' was faced. Why does the search for truth matter? Aspects of the growth of Nazism and the events of the last war, were also included.

A Lesson on 'Rush to Judgement'

I visited this teacher some time after he had completed the account of his use of the book with a fifth form. He was then using the book with a fourth-year mixed class, the third stream down out of four streams. This was one of the concluding lessons on the book and the class were divided into two sets, one of which had just begun considering all the evidence from the viewpoint of the Warren Commission, the other from the viewpoint of Mark Lane.

All the children had copies of the book and each group had at least one complete Jackdaw Folder.

What follows is a detailed account of what took place during that lesson.

The teacher began by reminding the class of the point they had reached on the previous day.

TEACHER: First Set (Warren Commission). Who? Why? How? Where?

Second Set (Mark Lane). Who? Why? How? Where? Angle?

76

Yesterday we were finding out the views of (1) The Warren Commission, and (2) Mark Lane. Who are they (the Warren Commission and Mark Lane)? What do they say? What are their views? Where do they get them from?

PUPIL: *Police and F.B.I.*

TEACHER: What is surprising about the investigations of the Commission?

PUPIL: *More time and money than Mark Lane, but they didn't sort out the same points.*

[At this point cards were passed round the groups. They had been made by the previous class, who had read the book as part of their C.S.E. course. They summarized effectively specific issues, e.g.

Why was Lee Harvey Oswald wanted?

The Assassination of President Kennedy—My Theories.

The Paraffin Test.

The Bullets—complete with very effective diagrams.]

TEACHER: *Warren Commission Group.* Find out who they were. Why? How long did they take?

Mark Lane Group. Find out who he is. What does he do? How does he get involved? When was his book published?

[The groups worked steadily at this for some fifteen minutes.]

TEACHER: Finish sentence you're on—pens down—look this way. I want to give you some further points—then you can finish.

Let's think about a murder mystery—film, TV play or book. If you were thinking of a recipe for this; what would it contain?

PUPIL: *Murder.*

TEACHER: What else?

PUPIL: *Victim.*

TEACHER: What kind of victim? Important or otherwise? Think (*pause*).

TEACHER: What else?

VARIOUS ANSWERS: *Weapon;*
Witnesses;
Murderer;
Clues;
Red herrings.

TEACHER: Let's compare the Kennedy assassination with the

perfect murder story. It has all the ingredients. What happened after the death of Kennedy which makes it even more mysterious?

PUPIL: *Tippit shot.*

TEACHER: Why was he there? He shouldn't have been there. What happened after that?

PUPIL: *Police converged to arrest Oswald.*

TEACHER: Where was he?

PUPIL: *In the cinema with a gun.*

[Discussion moved on to the killing of Oswald himself.]

TEACHER: Who did it? Was he a good patriotic man sympathetic to John Kennedy?

PUPIL: *Jack Ruby.*

TEACHER: A sleazy small-time gangster—knows two hundred police and so on. Why did he do it? Why did the police say he did it? Why did the Warren Commission say he did it?

PUPIL: *He did it for John Kennedy.*

TEACHER: But where was he at the time of the assassination?

PUPIL: *Planning a crooked deal in his club.*

TEACHER: What did he die of?

PUPIL: *Cancer.*

TEACHER: It's almost like a movie director's dream. Think of the number of people who witnessed the murder. Think of the mystery of Brennan. Think of the mystery of the police car that wasn't where it should have been. I'm trying to show you the doubts Mark Lane puts on it. But remember that this is his job—it's *his* job to cast doubts. Wait a minute —don't think of him as a knight in shining armour.

[Here followed a brief discussion of the Kennedy family and particularly of President Kennedy's background.]

TEACHER: Summary—rich, famous, he had known misery and grief. Happily married?

PUPIL: *Yes, to a very attractive woman.*

TEACHER: Try to imagine with all this how America went berserk. How everyone felt guilty! Another point. Does it matter who did it? Is truth important? Let's get away from murder. Does truth in anything matter? Let's imagine something simple. We all pinch Peter's book as a joke and we don't tell him. Does it matter? What effect does this have?

PUPIL: *He won't trust anyone any more.*

TEACHER: Go further—we all say the opposite of the truth for a week. What happens if there is no trust, if we can't rely on people?

ANSWER 1: *None of us trust anybody.*

ANSWER 2: *We go back to a savage.*

TEACHER: Exactly. Now do you think truth matters? What about censorship? How about Vietnam? Contrast the U.S. and North Vietnamese casualty figures. In a war, remember, it's someone's job to tell lies. Is this a good or bad thing? If you can't rely on the Government telling you the truth, is this a good or a bad thing? Can you think of any countries where lies have been told at some time?

[Various suggestions are put forward by the class.]

TEACHER: Every country. What if flying saucers have landed. What do we do?

[Pause—no reply from the class.]

TEACHER: It's difficult, isn't it! I'm glad you couldn't decide.

[The teacher went on to tell the class of the notorious Orson Welles 'War of the Worlds' broadcast and of the ensuing panic which swept America.]

TEACHER: Is the Government right to not tell the people?

PUPIL: *Yes.*

TEACHER: But I've talked you into it. Just now you said censorship was a bad thing. When you've finished the writing you're on, do these questions.

1. Does it matter who did it? or why?
2. Why the whole world mourned.

[Lesson ends]

Inevitably a great deal of the excitement and success of this lesson disappears once it is transcribed, but I hope that at least the flavour of it remains. It fully substantiated the claims the teacher made in his original description and indeed was one of the most lively, original and provocative 'English' lessons I have ever seen. The class was composed of exactly the kind of children some teachers dread teaching, but here they were all completely absorbed in what they were doing and

79

learning a great deal from it. Particularly noticeable is the skill with which the teacher draws on the children all the time, but leads them precisely in whatever direction he wants, in order to establish the points he wishes to make.

THE ASHWORTH GROWLER

John Kennett. (Dolphin Books. University of London Press) *used in conjunction with :*
SILVERTIP, Harper Cory, Dolphin Books, U.L.P.
THE WARRIOR'S TREASURE, R. J. McGregor, Dolphin Books, U.L.P.
ADVENTURES WITH A BOFFIN, Jean Marsh, Dolphin Books, U.L.P.
Age-range 12–13 (less able children—*The Ashworth Growler* is designed for a reading age of 9–10; the other three titles for a reading age of 10–11. Eight copies of each title were available)

The chief reason for the success of *The Ashworth Growler* is that it is easy to read and suits the reading age of the children for whom it is designed. The vocabulary of the book is limited to words which the children meet daily in their normal home environment and the story is based upon a very ordinary family with which the children can associate themselves. It contains the right amount of humour to sustain their interest —most of this of the very slapstick kind which children enjoy. Above all, although simple, it does not condescend to the readers for whom it is intended and the author has succeeded in meeting the needs of the children's reading and chronological ages. There are other factors which help—the book's presentation is attractive, the print large and clear enough, and the illustrations acceptable and sometimes quite amusing.

From the teaching point of view it also has the merit of being a useful springboard for all kinds of activities. As one secondary modern teacher I interviewed put it: 'I chose the book because it lent itself to branching out into wider aspects of living.' Or again, 'I choose my books according to the needs of my pupils and *The Ashworth Growler* satisfied the needs and desires of 2C to be stimulated.'

The same teacher felt, as did others concerned with rather different kinds of children, that, although this was a simple book which most adults could read easily in less than an hour, there was a value and a sense of achievement in persuading 2C to read it from cover to cover. He was also well aware of the limitations of the book, but felt that it was important to begin where the child is. 'I accept the fact that one progresses in literature as one progresses in other things. In the first place I use books which they can come to and they use and say, "Yes, this I know", and one wants some rapport at this level. One can take them on to books which ask them to know things outside their environments.' He saw the reading of 'real literature' as a goal which these children would have to be led slowly towards. He hoped that at least by the third or fourth year it would be possible to get them on to worthwhile contemporary books, e.g. *Lord of the Flies*.

Finally, he felt that it was important really to know his children before using the book with them ('The children come first and the choice of book comes second'), and that his success with the book lay not so much in the book itself, but in the way he had used it.

Treatment of the Book

I am most grateful to a Warwickshire teacher for allowing me to reproduce his account of the teaching of the book which follows. The book was used with a second-year mixed secondary modern class of twenty-seven children. It was the bottom stream of three streams and the book was used (in conjunction with three others) for roughly two periods a week over two terms. A small set of the book was used in turn by a group within the class and the book was read partly in class and partly at other times.

Method of reading

The greater part of the two lessons per week were given over to 'group reading' of the book. The group comprised seven pupils, boys and girls, each pupil reading a portion to the rest of the group. In this way, the pupils helped each other with difficult words and awkward phrases, calling me in only when there were impossible problems for them. I moved around the groups listening to pupils' reading and asking them questions designed to test their comprehension of the story and sequence of events. My questions also led the pupils on to broader areas of interest, perhaps only touched on by the book. Such areas investigated with regard to *this* book may be summarized thus:

1. The Highway Code and road sense.
2. Motor cars and vehicle manufacture.
3. Services for the motorist.
4. Traffic offences and their punishment.

The class and the book
At this point, and to avoid possible confusion, I should note that *The Ashworth Growler* was used in conjunction with three other books of the same calibre, the four being conveniently of approximately the same length. The other three books were:

Silvertip, Harper Cory
The Warrior's Treasure, R. J. McGregor
Adventures with a Boffin, Jean Marsh

The whole class was divided into four roughly equal groups and carefully balanced so that each group contained boys and girls, poor readers and better readers, precocious and withdrawn pupils, etc. Each group had its own reader, and each group as it finished one book 'swopped' it for one of the other books and contributed a fair amount of written and oral work.

The above facts must be known to assess the value of the next section. Although this questionnaire restricts me to one book, the same methods were applied to the other three books with modifications, of course, in topics to suit the contents of each individual book.

Oral work
In addition to oral work arising out of my 'intrusion' into the group's work, each group gave a periodic, oral report on its book, recounting to the rest of the class exciting or interesting incidents from the book, thus preparing the others for their own reading of it. As time went on and each group had read more than one of the titles, discussions arose from the different approach each group had to the same book.

Homework and projects for homework
1. A certain portion was set each week to be read individually and alone as homework.

2. Essays:

'Describe Mrs Ashworth's driving test—ask your mother or father for first-hand impressions to make your account more vivid.'

'Draw as many road signs as you can think of, explain carefully their location and their importance to road users.'

'Read the Highway Code—especially the section for motorists.'

In all honesty, written work on this and the other titles was generally disappointing—for me, the teacher, at any rate, but not necessarily so for the pupils. Written work never seemed to reflect adequately the pupils' enthusiasm for these books.

Written Work

The teacher himself states that he was disappointed in the standard of written work achieved by the class. Unfortunately, he did not have the time to put into practice his ideas about written work based upon the book, with this particular class. 'Had I had time, the ultimate product of my reading project would have been a folio containing fairly short essays written by a large number of children on both conventional and unconventional aspects of the story. I would have, in dealing with *The Ashworth Growler*, liked to take them [the children] down to my car and let them open the bonnet and work the gear lever, and start the car and merely back up the picture and sentence form in the back of the book. I would have liked to have arranged for somebody to come to the school to talk about Road Safety and Taking a Driving Test or I would have liked to have taken the children somewhere where they could have seen these things at first hand.'

Thus he feels that written work with these children must be linked to a practical activity, in other words, the writing about something is linked with the doing of it. Like the Hertford-shire teacher mentioned earlier, he makes, not quite so consciously perhaps, a plea for the integration of subject material and for involvement. 'It all ultimately boils down to the basic feeling I have about teaching C stream children. One forgets one is an English teacher and you teach these children the act of communication and the act of observation, and if this means poaching some of the Geography or History teacher's ground—fair enough.'

Thus all the writing done by these children was developing in a concrete way some of the wider areas of investigation already discovered and discussed in class. Conversely, any essays on any literary aspect of the books was beyond them and clearly a complete waste of everybody's time.

Brief Notes on Work Connected with the Other Books Used in the Scheme

1. *Silvertip*

   'Watch TV when a circus or a visit to the zoo is shown. From this try to get some ideas about animals in captivity, particularly whether you thought it was right?'

   This led directly into the situation in the children's own homes with their own pets which had once known freedom. In turn this developed into a consideration of the much wider issues of liberty and confinement (prison).

2. *The Warrior's Treasure*

   This is a school treasure-hunt story in which there turns out to be no treasure at all. Thus the book has a valuable message in the moral that you don't always get what you want out of life.

   Other books about treasure hunts (e.g. *Treasure Island*) were looked at for comparison and a current newspaper story about the exploration of a galleon was made use of.

3. *Adventures with a Boffin*

   Maps of India were used in trying to discover what sort of area the story is set in. The *Life Book of India* was also very useful in connection with this. This book has its dull patches —the children were very conscious of this and were 'bribed' through by discussion of the exciting bits, e.g. the accident where they are trapped in a pit. The book was also linked with J. H. Williams' *Elephant Bill*.

The Value of Group Work

I have already noted that this teacher felt that a large measure of his success with the book was due to the way he had used it, and he felt very strongly about the value of reading in groups, for this kind of child particularly.

As far as the mechanics of reading are concerned, there is a great chance of a child plodding away on his own, simply missing out the words he cannot read or does not understand. In a group, however, the other members will not allow this. His discipline was fairly strict—irrelevant chatter was not allowed, but this did not inhibit the purposeful discussions going on within each group. He was rightly convinced that what happened within each group was more educative and valuable an experience than the experience of the simple group reader itself.

I am interested in the learning process and I think children learn considerably more from each other than the teacher, because the relationship is less strange. They learn less easily from the formidable person in the front of the class. I am interested in teaching the skill of teaching and by working in a group the children teach each other—they will help each other. There is no use at all in my going along and saying, 'This word is "expedition".' [During the lesson at which I was present, a child had asked for this word to be explained. Rather than explain it himself, the teacher coaxed a very adequate explanation out of one of the other children in the group.] I think learning and knowledge have to come from within, one child teaching another child; their patience is greater than mine. It helps not only the child who learns the word, but also reinforces the knowledge of the child who tells them what it is. They get rid of me for two out of five lessons; they only see me passing through the groups and I can be more relaxed. There was freer discussion between themselves than there was with me. Once again, it is improving their oral expression, verbalizing their thoughts—this is the value of the group project.

For a further account of teaching with a less able class, see also the discussion of *Lord of the Flies*, page 54.

Chapter Five

MORE PRACTICE

Inevitably any detailed discussion of method and approaches has had to be limited to a small number of titles, representative of the age and ability range. This has meant that a number of interesting and useful accounts of work with other books have not been included. It would be a pity if some of these were not more widely available and I now reproduce therefore a representative sample of them. These accounts appear without comment and are taken from my original questionnaire. I am grateful to the teachers concerned for permission to reproduce them.

TOM SAWYER
Mark Twain. (Collins—available in various other editions)
Comprehensive school, North Midlands
Class 11 + (mixed, unstreamed. Book used for two periods in a week, for six weeks)

As the ability of the class ranged from below I.Q. 100 to above I.Q. 135, I felt it was necessary to make a strong impact at the beginning, so that the weaker readers would become sufficiently involved to *want* to read on and not be put off by some of the slight difficulties of the vocabulary and Twain's recording of the American accent. Obviously, the experience of the book had to find some response within the children's own experience. Before reading the book at all, we spent two or three lessons in the hall improvising around the idea of domineering adults, spoilt favourites (like Sid in the book), getting into mischief, etc. I followed this by reading aloud the first twenty pages or so, hoping that the standard of *my* reading would be higher than that of the class! and hoping to register some of the humour—a quality sometimes missed by the slower reader of this book.

My method for most of the book was to ask the class to reach a certain page by the next lesson to be given to *Tom Sawyer*, always trying to see that their set reading included one of the highspots of the book which would be worth discussion. I often split the class into groups of about five or six and asked them to discuss certain incidents and later report their views to the rest of the class. (For instance, one group might discuss the raid of Tom and Huck on the Sunday school picnic. Why do the boys make this raid? Who is the ringleader? Does it read like an ordinary, everyday event? Do you think Tom and Huck were *wrong* to do this?) Occasionally I would ask someone to prepare a reading of a few paragraphs they particularly enjoyed in the portion of the book set. (Incidentally, I tried hard not to discourage and bore the keener ones who had read quickly to the end, so I never spent a whole lesson 'reading on from the place we had reached'—there were too many 'places'.)

About every fourth lesson devoted to *Tom Sawyer* would be given to dramatizing incidents from the book, often extending the subject matter beyond the information on the pages: for example, the whole class acted the 'funeral' of the boys, and then split into smaller groups and made up scenes that might have happened if *they* had been involved in such an escapade, and how they would have been received at home afterwards. The aims of such dramatization are pretty obvious: to bring alive the incidents from the page and to try to get the pupils to evaluate the novel in terms of their own experience.

On about four occasions I used the book as a stimulus to creative writing; the Tom / Beckie Thatcher 'courtship' provided an opportunity for the pupils to write about times when they have shown off or had fights. The only writing of any critical form came after we had finished the book and the pupils were invited to write their reactions and observations in a diary in which they recorded their library reading and group readers. At this age only four or five pupils gave any real assessment of the book—other contributions varied from a three-line, 'I like it' to a four-page 'telling the story'.

Discussion usually wandered far from the text, with the pupils giving more or less relevant examples of their own experiences. The sort of question that usually provoked discussion would be one asking for explanation of a character's motive in a certain piece of behaviour, an opinion of the right or wrong in an issue, or an expression of whether the pupil would have behaved in that way.

REFERENT, a short story from *THE DAY IT RAINED FOR EVER*

Ray Bradbury. (Penguin Books)
Secondary modern school, Home Counties
Class 14+ (girls, fourth-year leavers. Story used for three periods in one week)

(This story, set in an educational institution in 1997, is concerned with the power of mind over matter and the way in which thought can change concepts and affect material objects.)

I entered the room and picked up a chair. I asked what it was. Response varied, but most seemed to believe I had gone mad, at last. I then asked how they knew it was a chair and arrived at some brief but interesting discussion. I suggested it was a battering ram, the agitator from a washing machine, headgear for carrying goods in a tropical land. My point was almost made when the girls began to make their own suggestions —a cradle, a barrow for a supermarket, etc.

I then drew a joined squiggle on the board and asked what it was. After consideration, ideas were forthcoming. Soon each suggestion was followed by an explanation by the inventor and a chorus of 'Oh, yeah' or 'Eh?' In the latter case the explanation was continued. The girls admitted that they could be convinced that several people in turn were correct because no real shape belonged to the object until a convincing argument was used.

When we reached this point, I read the story. Several of the points arising were discussed, but mainly that of how we could limit the use of something by being sure of its purpose.

Dramatic work followed individually, in pairs and in groups. The girls were asked to show with their bodies that they were holding one object which gradually changed into something quite different. Most did so effectively—many too quickly—and without self-consciousness. Pairs then planned the handing over of objects which changed and had to plan the way in which they could work together to make their point.

The ultimate object was to write a story called 'The Change'. While several of the tales were hurried and puerile, some had considerable force and the great majority worked well!

THE HISTORY OF MR POLLY
H. G. Wells. (Collins Classics)
Grammar school, North-West
Class 14 + (boys, 'Express' stream taking 'O' level in four years. Book used for about thirty periods)

The boys had had the texts for some time before formal work began and had been recommended to read them privately. When formal work began, they were given a fortnight in which to read the book privately, out of class. Meanwhile, in class, I began a series of readings in which I read aloud selected passages: Mr Polly's education; the funeral; the idyll with Christabel; the wedding; the fight with Rusper; The Great Fire of Fishbourne; acceptance at the Potwell Inn; the war with Uncle Jim; Miriam revisited; Conclusion. The readings were evenly spaced throughout the period of study, each with its follow-up lesson, and an essay when there was material enough for one to be written.

The readings were performances punctuated with comments made 'aside', heavy emphasis here and there, significant silences, winks, gestures, facial expressions, etc. They were intended to draw attention to the contradictions inherent in Mr Polly's potential as a person and his education, his longing for noble conduct and acceptance of the inferior, his assertion of individuality against crowding circumstances, the final triumph of his sense of right over the promptings of self-interest. They were also intended to render the sound of comic dialogue and hilarious narrative, the sound of zest for life and the sound of Wells's ironic comments, both explicit and implicit.

The follow-up lesson to each reading usually began with my asking: 'What do you want to know?' As far as possible I nudged the boys into answering their own or each other's questions. When necessary I gave short talks on subjects like

89

nineteenth-century education in England, the economics of keeping a small shop, the landscape of South-East England before the motor car, and I also proffered fragments of information about such things as the significance of bicycles in late nineteenth-century England, the niceties of the wedding ritual, the language of military history (with reference to the war with Uncle Jim), nineteenth-century liquor licensing laws, etc. As far as possible I saw to it that the information was elicited from me by questions. I recommended further reading to supplement my answers.

At appropriate intervals essays were set on: (1) What went wrong with Mr Polly's education or father's funeral or idyll with Christabel or wedding or shopkeeping. (2) The trouble with Miriam. (3) Mr Polly and his neighbours. (4) Violent conflict (dismissal of Parsons, fight with Rusper, or war with Uncle Jim). The essays were written partly in class, when I was available for advice, partly outside class for homework. I gave a generous allowance of time (say two lessons and two half-hour periods of homework), and expected 700–800 words, well composed and handsomely presented. There were follow-up lessons for explanations, recriminations, elucidations and further discussion.

Non-literary lessons were allowed to grow out of these follow-up lessons. As the boys felt the need, in writing their essays, of a technique more economical than that of rewriting narrative or dialogue verbatim, I offered them formal instruction in summary. Similarly, as the need for flexible, succinct modes of expression were felt, I taught quite sophisticated techniques of reported speech. Other matters were the presentation of quotations, methods of reference, and the layout of the page. Probably the most important non-literary work arising out of the study of the book was that on the organizing of arguments into a simple pattern of assertion, evidence, explanation, conclusion.

The development of these lessons on technique was not entirely fortuitous. I intended that they should be given during the term in which they were given, but the times at which they were given depended on when the boys felt the need for them. Sometimes it was necessary to create a need, e.g. for the lessons on the organizing of arguments.

It was all much less methodical, much more casual, than it sounds here. I knew what I wanted to do in the time available: the readings, the essays, the lessons on technique. But I did not plan rigidly, or predetermine the course of a lesson. As I did not normally read aloud for more than twenty-five minutes in any one lesson, questioning and discussion merged into the readings and served as links between them. In discussion the boys contributed a lot of information, e.g. about bicycles, about shops kept by parents or acquaintances, about funerals and weddings, etc.

At first the boys did not know what questions to ask, and had to be prompted. In the earlier lessons they contented themselves with factual questions (e.g. 'What does Wells mean when he says . . .?' or 'What was a National School?'). They progressed to questions of moral or literary significance (e.g. 'What did Mr Polly want to go and visit Miriam for at the end? She was only a nuisance to him' or 'What was so wonderful about Boccaccio?' or 'Why does Wells have Uncle Pentstemon in the story at all?'). In the final stages they would question my and each other's interpretations and offer their own (e.g. 'Aren't you a bit hard on Uncle Jim? He never had much of a chance, and after all it was his own auntie, so he ought to be able to borrow off her' or 'Aren't you making Mrs Larkins sound too low class when you read it like that? I think she tries to be respectable, because . . .').

The characteristic feature of the work was the readings, in which I tried to relate the printed words to the sound of human voices. The characteristic situation was rather like that in a theatre: the relationship I sought was comparable with that between actor and audience.

THE IDES OF MARCH
Thornton Wilder. (Penguin Books)
Public school, West of England
Class 15+ (boys, unstreamed. Book used (in conjunction with others) for six periods a week for six weeks)

This was read in conjunction with a number of other books, all of which were intended to provide a background to the acting/reading of Shakespeare's *Julius Caesar*. Other works included: *Young Caesar / Imperial Caesar* (Rex Warner), *Caesar and Cleopatra* (G. B. Shaw), *Plutarch's Lives, Suetonius, Cicero's Letters* (where relevant), a selection of the poems of *Catullus*.

91

For modern parallels: *The Last Days of Hitler* (H. R. Trevor-Roper).

The class divided itself into small groups of two, three or four, and each group undertook a project concerned with a character in Wilder's imaginative reconstruction of Caesar's Rome, e.g. a typical project—*Cicero* (three boys taking part: one of whom concentrated on Cicero's letters, comparing the originals with Wilder's imaginary letters; another dealing with the particular character traits revealed by Wilder's portrait; and another with Cicero's relationship to the other characters —his place in the jigsaw). The project was presented as a fifteen-minute broadcast, each boy being responsible for five minutes 'on the air'. At the end of the 'programme'—the 'public' (i.e. the rest of the class) would be invited to discuss the presentation given and to question the producers/performers on their use of illustrative material. Multiply this sort of project by seven and you have a fair idea of the teaching approaches used.

Using Wilder as a springboard we went on to study Shakespeare's use of sources. First, reading a passage in *Plutarch*; then getting the class to dramatize the passage; having done this, turning to Shakespeare. (I find this an effective way of demonstrating the power of Shakespeare's architectonic imagination.)

Boys were also invited to contribute letters, etc., to an enlarged edition of Wilder's *The Ides of March*.[1]

CIDER WITH ROSIE
Laurie Lee. (Penguin Books)
Comprehensive school, London
Class 15 + (girls, unstreamed. Book used for approximately two periods a week for seven weeks)

As this is a C.S.E. set book I planned to read it as part of a half-term's project on 'Childhood' which would allow the book to be the starting point and framework, but also allow the introduction of a great deal of related material, visual as well as literary. Time was divided roughly into two periods a week for actual reading and talk about the book, two for related material, largely introduced by me as the starting point

---

[1] See also page 100 for an account of the rest of the year's work with this class for 'O' level G.C.E.

for written work and discussion, and two periods for group work on the project itself.

The first chapters I read aloud to the class. The whole book has not been read in class in this way, but I wanted to begin with a shared experience in order to establish the kind of discussion I wanted and to allow the project to grow quite naturally from the shared discussion about Laurie Lee's earliest memories and the girls' own related experiences. I tried to direct discussion to a fairly specific examination of the child's growing awareness of his environment and the way Laurie Lee describes his gradual development. From particular discussion of the text we moved to the girls' own early memories and their observation of younger children. The first piece of written work arose from a specific consideration of Laurie Lee's description of the grass jungle the three-year-old finds himself in at the beginning of the book. We considered the world as it must appear to the three-year-old, and they wrote either from their own early memories or described the possible experience of a small child in the everyday, but outsize, world—a child's-eye view of familiar objects or places.

From their discussion and from the quality of written work, I felt that I could now introduce the project. I suggested that they should look at the way children grow and develop between birth and school age—further if they wished. I explained that much visual material would be available—chiefly colour supplements, old magazines, etc., for them to use as they wished—asked them to use library, public libraries, own families, snapshots of themselves where possible, and directed attention to Penguin psychology books, e.g. Winnicott, Hadfield, and a number of autobiographical novels available as small sets. I also explained that I would use one double period a week in which I would introduce related material myself, for discussion and written work which might help them to establish the direction of their own group enquiry. They were quite free to choose the method of presentation. Various groups (two to six girls in each) chose:

Wall displays, using appropriate visual material and a variety of types of writing, factual, informative, imaginative, etc.

Tape-recording—programme 'Babies' information poems, readings from own work and extracts from books.

Group folder or scrap book.

The girls' general approach was influenced by a series in the *Sunday Times* supplement on child development—but largely directed by material introduced by me which encouraged exploration of specific topics. No time limit was imposed— the most valuable aspect of these lessons was the detailed discussion taking place in the groups rather than the end product itself.

Material introduced by me
The relationship of the material used in these lessons to *Cider with Rosie* and the girls' own projects was always carefully discussed. I arranged the work under fairly general themes as follows:

INTRODUCTORY THEME

Birth: Read extract from *The Rainbow* (D. H. Lawrence)—Anna and father's reaction to birth of baby. 'Baby Running across the Grass', poem by D. H. Lawrence. Two Chinese poems (Po Chu I), a father's thoughts about baby.
Discussion:
  1. Exploratory, specific discussion of passage and poems.
  2. General talk about own experiences of birth.
Writing: Chiefly poems about birth, or the world of the baby— the less able found pictures of babies a great help for detailed observation.

GROWING AWARENESS OF ENVIRONMENT

1. Discussion of Laurie Lee's own discoveries about the world beyond home and family. Class selected own examples from text.
2. *B.B.C. Books, Plays and Poems—God Made Sunday* (Walter Macken). Listened to extract in which small boy is first aware of another person as a personality distinct from himself.
3. Talk about child's developing concept of self through contact and conflict with others—drawing largely on girls' own memories.
4. In next lesson on this theme read extract from *Aaron's Rod* (D. H. Lawrence), *The Blue Ball* (printed in *Things Being Various*, Clements, Dixon, Stratta).

5. *The Blue Ball* is a splendid stimulus for talk and writing
about the ambivalent relationship between siblings (looked
back to Laurie Lee's own attitude to sisters and younger
brothers—a far more objective and distant account than
D. H. Lawrence's) *and* between parent and child. The girls
were particularly interested and perceptive about Milli-
cent's domineering attitude to her sister and her desire to
destroy the blue ball which had been her father's. There
was much very thoughtful talk about a child's growing
awareness of himself in relation to others, a child's need to
identify with possessions, the need to challenge authority
and in particular to test parental love in a jealous need for
the assurance of the totality of this love. The girls drew
these very powerful themes from this extract and seemed
anxious to establish some satisfactory explanation for the
frequent perverse and disruptive behaviour they had
observed in small children. They discussed the effects of
insecurity and other kinds of deprivation on the development of a child as a social being. Their discussion at this
point was very controlled and mature! I think because they
felt able to draw on their own experience (in relation to the
extract) in a rather formal, clinical way.

PLAY, IMAGINATION AND FANTASY

(These headings were for my own use only and *not* given to the
children, only I hope rather vaguely deduced by them from
the slant I gave the material.)

Read:
   'A Child Is Singing', poem by Adrian Mitchell (*Here Today*).
Discussion: The way children explore and come to terms with
   world through play and explanatory talk about games—
   direct link with game Laurie Lee's brother is playing in the
   chapter 'The Kitchen'—in both poem and game the deep-
   rooted fears of childhood emerge in repetitive chanting.
   Direct discussion and description of own brothers' and
   sisters' games. This led to talk about the fantasies and fears
   which are often subject of child's play, with specific reference
   to Laurie Lee's own fantasies and fears in the chapter 'First
   Names'.
Writing: Of very high quality at this point. Listened to another
   extract from *God Made Sunday* in which the children act a
   play for adult audience which is a failure.

Discussion : Inevitability of child's attempts to enter adult world and achieve adult standards and subsequent distress at failure. Girls talked about similar attempts and own experiance of adults' dishonest response to their efforts.

FRIENDSHIP

Re-read Laurie Lee's own experience in *Village School*, compared this with William Saroyan story, *B.B.C. Listening and Writing Series*, also read and discussed quarrel which takes place at the beginning of *There Is a Happy Land* by Keith Waterhouse.

Discussion : Own early friendships. At this point I would have liked a visit to a local nursery school for direct observation —but it wasn't possible at the time. Similar treatment of other themes directly suggested by the book was carried out, e.g. misbehaviour and punishment, mothers' relations, sickness in childhood.

All the themes of course overlap all the time and involve continual reference back to *Cider with Rosie*. In addition to class work each girl was given a worksheet designed to give help with general reading or revision. The questions are not designed to encourage the collection of factual information, but as a guide to the central issues in each chapter. These sheets are useful only in so far as they are used as a guide for the weaker readers or as comprehension practice which can easily be set if the class teacher is absent. Many of the girls seem to gain satisfaction from answering the questions and handing them in to be marked, in their own time.

At the same time the girls are being encouraged to read as widely as possible from a selection of books including many autobiographical novels, e.g.

Dandelion Days, Henry Williamson
The Member of the Wedding, Carson McCullers
African Child, Camara Laye
A Portrait of the Artist as a Young Man, James Joyce
To Kill a Mocking Bird, Harper Lee
Through the Tunnel, Lessing, and *A Message from the Pigman*, Wain, from *Short Stories of Our Time*

SAMPLE FROM WORKSHEET USED WITH 'CIDER WITH ROSIE'

First light
1. Why do you think the boy was so frightened when the family arrived in their new home?
2. How did the girls and their mother react to their new home?
3. As the little boy grows he begins to make discoveries about his new world. Make a list of some of these.
4. Explain the mystery of the 'stranger'.
5. What was home like when mother went to visit father?
6. What impression of this family and their life do you get from this chapter?

Village school
1. Why was Laurie Lee disappointed by his first day at school?
2. Describe the difference between the Infants' and the Big Room. Why did Laurie prefer to be in the Infants' Room?
3. What is Crabby like as a teacher? How did she differ from the new teacher?
4. List some of the details of school life which Laurie Lee remembers with pleasure.

Mother
1. Why did the school teacher take an interest in Laurie's mother and why were his efforts wasted?
2. What do you learn about the life of a girl in domestic service at this time and why do you think Laurie Lee's mother enjoyed it?
3. Why was his mother a 'lonely young woman'?
4. Why do you think her husband left her? How does she feel about him?
5. Why was the family always in financial trouble?
6. Do you find Laurie Lee's mother a likeable person? Describe at least three different things Laurie Lee tells us about her which show how much she enjoyed life. What do you think he learnt from her?

Chapter Six

LIVING WITH 'O' LEVEL LITERATURE

Most of the teachers I interviewed who were concerned with 'O' level Literature were not very happy about the examination. Some objected to the restrictions imposed by 'set books', others found the books set adequate, but complained that the questions set in the examination were often a test of memory and not of a real response to the books. Some teachers suggested that the situation could be very easily and rapidly improved if there were only some connections or pattern in the books which were set—thus making a coherent study. Nearly all were unhappy about the false distinction between language and literature which the system imposed. Perhaps the greatest condemnation came from the Head of Department in a comprehensive school who, in explaining why his school did not do 'O' level Literature at all in the fifth year, remarked, 'The major reason is that you can do more literature in the fifth year if you don't do Literature!'

At the same time, it must in fairness be said that a small number of the teachers I interviewed felt that the examinations had improved over the years, that the books chosen were suitable and that the questions set on them were fair enough. They also claimed that the examination did not alter their own teaching methods—this was certainly true, but they themselves were exceptionally able teachers and I doubt very much if the same is true of their less able and perhaps less confident colleagues.

However, there is little point in here going on into a detailed consideration of the objections to the present system—

chiefly because it has been done very ably elsewhere. Those particularly interested in the case against the traditional G.C.E. are referred to the following:

The Examining of English Language, S.S.E.C., H.M.S.O., 1964
English Examined—A Survey of 'O' Level Papers, N.A.T.E.
  (This substantial pamphlet consists of a National Survey of both Language and Literature papers and includes details of some experimental syllabuses.)
Examinations in English Literature at 'O' Level, a Report by a working party of the Birmingham N.A.T.E./Use of English Group. (This is an impressively thorough, detailed and constructive critique. It contains an informed and impassioned introductory statement on the objections to the present system and an evaluation of many of the Literature papers actually set in 1965 and 1966. It also includes a suggested Specimen Syllabus for Literature at 'O' level.)

Let us now turn more positively to two current experiments which I came across and which give some cause for hope.

1. *Oxford and Cambridge Schools' Examination Board. Experiment in 'O' Level English Literature, 1968*

This experiment was set up by the Board, working in conjunction with a number of boys' public schools.

The examination consists of:

(i) *An assessment by the school of a term's work* (60 marks)

The syllabus for this part of the examination is devised by the school and may be varied from class to class.

N.B. The work is assessed entirely by the school—no external moderation.

(ii) *An essay of 1500 to 2000 words on a book or books or literary topic or topics which may be the same as or related to those studied in (i) above* (40 marks)

The subject or subjects of the essay are chosen by the school. The essay is marked by the school and submitted for external moderation.

99

(iii) *Either Paper I or Paper III from the normal regulations of the Board*

This paper will continue to be set, marked and awarded by the Board. There will be a hurdle of forty-five per cent in this part of the examination.

The schools concerned in this experiment took full advantage of the freedom it afforded. Thus in addition to preparation for the Board's paper on Shakespeare's *Julius Caesar* one teacher forecast his work for two terms as follows:

Patterns of childhood (Christmas and Spring terms)
A study of:

George Eliot, *The Mill on the Floss*
Henry James, *The Turn of the Screw*
William Golding, *Lord of the Flies*
J. D. Salinger, *Catcher in the Rye*

In addition an anthology of poetry will be compiled—including original work.

The list of secondary reading—where free choice will be given—will include:

Harper Lee, *To Kill a Mockingbird*
Charles Dickens, *David Copperfield*
J. S. Mill, *Autobiography*
Richard Hughes, *A High Wind in Jamaica*
Jeremy Sandford, *Cathy Come Home*
William Wordsworth, *The Prelude (Book I)*

Another class in the same school, in addition to the work on *Julius Caesar*, spent the Christmas term in assessing the varying characteristics of Shakespeare's kings (*Richard II*, *Henry IV (I) and (II)* and *Henry V*). The Spring term was spent in a detailed comparative study of H. G. Wells's *Kipps* and George Orwell's *Keep the Aspidistra Flying*. 'We shall try to contrast Kipps and Gordon Comstock—the innocent who adores money and middle-class values and the rebellious member of the middle class who deliberately rejects the very things which Kipps cherishes.'

In another school taking part in the same scheme, the boys in the Autumn term worked on *The Ides of March* (as already described on page 91) and other books, as an introduction to *Julius Caesar*. They also did a modern-dress production of the play for the boys in the school, to which they could invite their friends. In the Spring term the class attempted general projects on science fiction, reading six to ten novels. Their teacher described the term's work as follows.

I bought batches of five books and the boys made their choice, also using anthologies of short stories and the common book *Second Orbit*. We are covering common ground with *Brave New World* (Aldous Huxley) and *1984* (George Orwell), leading up to Ray Bradbury's *The Day it Rained for Ever*, John Wyndham's *The Chrysalids*, *The Drowned World* (J. G. Ballard), *The Black Cloud* (Fred Hoyle), *Penguin Science Fiction* (ed. Brian Aldiss), *More Penguin Science Fiction* (ed. Brian Aldiss), and Brian Aldiss's *Introducing Science Fiction* (Faber). We had a central book exchange with a fairly constant circulation of titles:

1. They read without any holds barred for three weeks.
2. Then they went into groups of three or four for discussions. I went round and joined in the discussions for a week.
3. For the next fortnight they worked on group projects— they did science fiction stories, plays, scenarios and broadcast plays.
4. They did something quite different for a week. All the time this work was going on they had two poetry lessons per week to keep them sane!
5. Then they had a week where they read their things and discussed them. They produced a tape of MacNeice's *The Dark Tower* after some background reading of *The Quest*. We took over the chapel, using the organ and drums. I was very surprised at how well it went.

During the two lessons of poetry we did (1) reading and discussing poems, (2) reading and discussing what they'd done in the last period. Then we started with animal observations, moving on to fictitious animals, real and fictitious people. I wanted them to get down to some really detailed descriptive writing.

Project work: They did individual bits called 'Vision of the Future', in which they were free to do as they liked. They could do it in the form of a journal, play, poem. We compared the different visions of the future; the writing was much more creative than critical.

From these three examples, the liberating effect of this experiment should be apparent. From the year's work of the last class alone, embracing as it does classical literature (in the strict sense), Shakespeare, science fiction and modern poetic drama, one senses a freedom and a zest quite unattainable under the restrictions of a limited number of set books.

One could still quibble perhaps. The retention by the Board of Paper I or Paper III, with an insistence that at least forty-five per cent marks are obtained on this paper, means that the Board still very directly and externally controls half the marks awarded. On the other hand, much of the work covered is left totally to the discretion of the school and thirty per cent of the total marks are based entirely upon the assessment of the school of its own part of the syllabus, and this is done without any external moderation of any kind.

Thus whatever teething troubles this experiment may produce, one must commend the initiative of the schools concerned and of the Oxford and Cambridge Board, and hope that the adoption of this kind of scheme can become far more widespread. The interesting work being done is proof enough of its value.

2. *Joint Matriculation Board's Experiment in the Assessment of English Language*

The Joint Matriculation Board has been running an experiment in the assessment of English Language in conjunction with a group of northern grammar schools since 1964–5. I ought at once to point out, before I am accused of irrelevance, that since the control of the syllabus is entirely in the hands of the participating schools, and since they are agreed that English teaching should be largely literature based, it would be more accurate under present divisions of the subject to call the syllabuses that I have seen English Literature. However, if this were done, the pupils concerned, however gifted, would fail to matriculate! The whole scheme is thus incidentally one more argument for the abolition of the Language/Literature division and for an examination/assessment in English.

Basically, the schools taking part draw up and teach their own syllabuses and their work is assessed and moderated by the Board. There are no external examinations and the Board has no control at all over the syllabuses followed by the schools. It is thus very similar to many C.S.E. Mode 3 schemes.

The Board has so far published two pamphlets on the scheme. The first (*English Language: an experiment in school assessing (first interim report)* by E. A. Hewitt and D. I. Gordon, J.M.B. occasional publication, 22 December 1965) is concerned entirely with the fairly complex practical procedure of assessment and moderation. It would, incidentally, also be of interest to those concerned with C.S.E. Mode 3 examining.

The second (*English Language: an experiment in school assessing (second interim report)*[1] by J. A. Petch, J.M.B. occasional publication, 26 July 1967) is perhaps of more general interest. It summarizes yet again the objections which many teachers have to the traditional examinations and goes on to give a general account of teaching under the experiment, based upon accounts received from the participating schools.

From this account it would seem that the effect of the experiment has been entirely good. It has resulted in wider reading directed towards particular topics such as Youth and the Social Order; Isolated Man; Professional Sport; and Advertising. It has created more opportunities for oral work and a thorough discussion closely united with what was being read, and a great deal of freer and wider written work has emerged from this discussion. Finally, as a result of this coherent approach to reading, talking and writing, the peripheral skills of English (punctuation, grammar, etc.) have been tackled in the meaningful context of each individual's writing. (The detailed account in the Board's pamphlet is well worth close study by any teacher concerned with or about G.C.E. English.)

Certainly, in the school I was able to visit one felt the same kind of liberated exhilaration as was present in the school undertaking the Oxford and Cambridge scheme. This school

---

[1] Both these pamphlets may be obtained, free and post free, on application in writing to the Secretary of the Board.

had been in the J.M.B. scheme from the beginning (four years) and the Head of the department commented, 'Over the four years we have become more and more free ourselves—we started with a terrible hangover of things which we felt we must do.'

This school took no other English examination. (I feel it is a pity and perhaps damaging to the scheme as a whole that some of the participating schools still found it necessary to take the traditional 'O' level Literature paper as well.) The Head of the department also stressed the unity of the subject that was now possible and the wider reading that went on. A great deal of the written work in the school was now based directly or indirectly upon the literature. She also found, as many C.S.E. groups have done, that the meetings with her colleagues for the purposes of assessment were of great general value. They had in fact become a vital forum for the exchange and transmission of ideas and for the broadening of everyone's outlook.

About what the scheme had done for her own department, she had this to say:

The change in our own attitude is subtle and hard to define. One member of the Department, who did her first teaching at Upper Fifth level as the project began, has found the scheme very valuable in that it obliged her to think out her own aims instead of blindly accepting a course labelled ' "O" level English Language'. We have always believed that English should be enjoyable, that the study of literature provides a valuable discipline, that the best way to improve one's writing is to write. Now all this is being demonstrated in our project work, and we can therefore with greater conviction apply these standards in the rest of the school. In all our teaching, our emphasis is now more firmly than ever on reading literature, on discussion, and on continuous writing.

The J.M.B. is to be warmly congratulated on pioneering such a promising path to reform. Clearly the most practical and positive step which any teacher finding it difficult to live with the more traditional 'O' level Literature can take is to contact either the Oxford and Cambridge or the Joint Matriculation Board and ask to join one or other of these schemes. An overwhelming amount of teacher support and interest would encourage the Boards in these experiments. It would also force them to rapidly consider how such schemes of examining might be made more widely available. Further, if enough teachers deserted the Boards offering only the traditional kind of examination, these Boards might eventually be forced into considering alternative methods.

Chapter Seven

SOME PARTING SHOTS

This has not been primarily an investigation of a statistical or factual nature and indeed the relevance of such an investigation to the actual practice of literature teaching would seem to me to be doubtful. It is thus not possible to draw the kind of conclusion based upon irrefutable statistical evidence that such an investigation would lead to.

However, certain points seem to be worth making, or, in some cases, re-making. Despite McLuhan's prognostications and those English teachers to whom the whole concept of a common reader is abhorrent, there is no doubt of the important and sometimes very central place which the class reader still has in most English teachers' conception of English teaching.

While my own investigation was in progress, the final report of a very thorough and complete investigation, by an expert American team, into the teaching of English in selected British secondary schools, appeared.[1] While not necessarily concerned with the same schools and teachers as I was (although there was some overlap), one of their findings is very relevant to this Report. Teachers were asked to rate the importance of twenty-three different kinds of teaching aid and material.

The ratings received for 'Class Sets of Books' were as follows:

Essential 56 per cent
Very Important 21·3 per cent
Of Some Importance 19·1 per cent

[1] *A Study of the Teaching of English in Selected British Secondary Schools*, U.S. Department of Health, Education and Welfare, February 1968.

Not Very Important 3·6 per cent
Detrimental to Good Teaching 0·0 per cent

Clearly some of the teachers who wrote to me condemning
the use of the class reader were not covered by this American
investigation! However, the American figures indicate that
those who have at least some doubts about its use may be
roughly twenty-three per cent. What is more significant, in
view of what many of the doubters claim, is that the 'Class Set
of Books' received a higher 'Essential' rating (fifty-six per cent)
than any other individual teaching aid habitually used by
teachers of English, while those firmly committed to the class
reader are roughly seventy-seven per cent.

If there is a good deal of agreement about the central place
of the class reader, there is a good deal less about what that
reader should be. The complete list of all books reported on
(Appendix C) shows a large number of books currently in use,
while the list of the books about which five or more questionnaires were received (Appendix B) is surprisingly short. One
would have expected perhaps a concentration on certain
favourites. It could be that the great diversity shown is a sign of
health, of a great deal of individual initiative and experiment.
It could also be that none of us yet know enough about what
kinds of books our children ought to be reading at any particular stage, in terms of their own growth and development.

Yet there is a sense, too, in which the teacher is more important than the book and in an investigation of this kind it
is impossible to separate the two. Many of the outstanding
teachers I met could have taught almost any book successfully
and most teachers feel that they can achieve a greater degree of
success with material that they themselves feel strongly about.
I am very conscious that in attempting to describe any teaching
experience on paper I am leaving the personality of the
teacher concerned out of the account. Yet this is probably the
most important single factor in the situation. For this reason,
therefore, anyone who regards these accounts as they stand as
blueprints for successful practice is going to come seriously
unstuck. To borrow a phrase from one of the teachers I interviewed, they are 'points of departure'.

At the same time, I hope that these examples of good practice will give the inexperienced or student teacher detailed and practical assistance of a kind that is often lacking. I have already noted two areas which those responsible for teacher training apparently need to take more account of. The ability to read aloud well and the ability to lead into a text using a dramatic approach are two essential and basic skills which English teachers often seem to lack.

There is another area to which I would like to draw attention. The development of an integrated curriculum, together with such techniques as team teaching, is to be welcomed for all kinds of reasons, some of which I have touched upon, particularly in thinking of less able children. It seems to me that there is a danger here that some English teachers may too readily forget what their own role in any such scheme ought to be. Some teachers, even in their own projects based upon their own class readers, in some of their activities too readily abandon what ought to be their special concerns, for those more properly belonging to their colleagues.

For if we cannot see that as English teachers, primarily concerned with the spoken and written word, we have a unique contribution to make to secondary education, however that education is organized, then we deserve to become the second-rate social scientists of a post-McLuhan era that some already see us as.

But what has Literature to contribute? It is time that we began to look very hard at the claims we continually make. What solid evidence have we for the kind of assumptions made in Chapter Two of this Report? We all need to know the answers.

Appendices

Appendix A

SOME CHILDREN'S REACTION TO SOME BOOKS

Wherever possible in the schools which were visited, the children who had read the books were asked to place them on the following five-point rating scale.

I enjoyed reading this book very much.
On the whole I enjoyed reading this book.
I did not particularly like or dislike reading this book.
On the whole I disliked reading this book.
I thoroughly disliked reading this book.

In order to obtain as accurate a response as possible, this test was administered by the research officer; the teacher who had taught the book was not present and it was made very clear that their individual reactions would not be divulged to their teachers or to the school.

The test was designed simply as a check upon the teacher's judgement and to ensure that children did in fact enjoy the books as their teachers claimed.

Clearly it would be foolish to draw any general conclusions from a comparatively small sample of something over 1000 children. It was, furthermore, a sample which could not be described as 'typical' or 'average' in that their teachers had themselves produced exceptional questionnaires, which had resulted in my visit.

However, within these limitations, it is apparent from the tabled results that:

1. Most children enjoyed the books which their teachers said they enjoyed. While clearly some children and some classes enjoyed a book more than others, their reaction was nearly always on the positive side of the mean. Only rarely did a child state that he or she disliked reading the book.

111

2. While it is clear that boys and girls in mixed classes did not usually enjoy the same book to the same extent (e.g. on the whole the boys enjoyed *Lord of the Flies* rather more than the girls did), the total reaction of the boys and the total reaction of the girls, to whatever book they were reading in whatever circumstances, was remarkably similar.

Note
In the 'Table of Results' which follows, the following abbreviations have been used in classifying the schools:

Ind.	= Independent
Ind. B.P.	= Independent Boys' Public
Ind. B.Pr.	= Independent Boys' Preparatory
G	= Grammar
G (D.G.)	= Direct Grant Grammar
G (V.A.)	= Voluntary Aided Grammar
Comp.	= Comprehensive
S/M	= Secondary Modern

The per cent figure in the last column represents the total reaction of the class as a percentage, e.g. if all the children in the class had given the book the top rating, the last column would read 100.

SOME CHILDREN'S REACTION TO SOME BOOKS

TABLE OF RESULTS

BOOK TITLE	SCHOOL	AGE	STREAM	SEX	NO. IN CLASS	MEAN	STANDARD DEVIATION	PER CENT
Animal Farm	G (D.G.)	14	None	Girls	29	2·90	0·82	72·4
Animal Farm	G	13	1/4	Boys	26	3·19	0·69	79·8
Animal Farm	S/M	15	2/2	Mixed	14	2·64	0·93	66·1
				Boys	9	2·56	0·73	63·9
				Girls	5	2·80	1·30	70·0
Lord of the Flies	G	15	1/4	Boys	26	3·46	0·81	86·5
Lord of the Flies	Comp.	14	1/4	Mixed	25	2·60	0·76	65·0
				Boys	13	2·46	0·78	61·5
				Girls	12	2·75	0·75	68·8
Lord of the Flies	S/M	14	6/6	Mixed	14	3·29	0·73	82·1
				Boys	9	3·44	0·53	86·1
				Girls	5	3·00	1·00	75·0

BOOK TITLE	SCHOOL	AGE	STREAM	SEX	NO. IN CLASS	MEAN	STANDARD DEVIATION	PER CENT
Lord of the Flies	S/M	14	2/4	Mixed	31	3·00	1·03	75·0
				Boys	15	3·20	0·94	80·0
				Girls	16	2·81	1·11	70·3
Lord of the Flies	Comp.	13	2/5	Mixed	26	2·58	1·03	64·4
				Boys	12	3·25	0·62	81·3
				Girls	14	2·00	0·96	50·0
Lord of the Flies	G (V.A.)	15	2/2	Boys	24	2·96	0·81	74·0
Far from the Madding Crowd	G	14	1/2	Girls	10	3·30	0·48	82·5
Short Stories of Our Time	G	15	None	Mixed	25	2·68	0·56	67·0
				Boys	15	2·47	0·52	61·7
				Girls	10	3·00	0·47	75·0
Short Stories of Our Time	S/M	15	1/2	Girls	32	2·50	0·72	62·5
'The Children' (*Walkabout*)	Comp.	13	2/12	Mixed	26	2·85	0·88	71·2
				Boys	15	2·67	1·05	66·7
				Girls	11	3·09	0·54	77·3

	Comp.							
'The Children' (*Walkabout*)		13	4/13	Mixed	31	2·45	0·77	61·3
				Boys	19	2·26	0·87	56·6
				Girls	12	2·75	0·45	68·8
Mill on the Floss	S/M	14	1/5	Mixed	23	2·09	1·08	52·2
				Boys	13	1·39	0·96	34·6
				Girls	10	3·00	0·00	75·0
Night Cargoes	S/M	12	2/6	Mixed	30	3·30	0·70	82·5
				Boys	12	3·33	0·65	83·3
				Girls	18	3·28	0·75	81·9
Tom Sawyer	S/M	11	1/5	Mixed	29	3·00	0·78	74·1
				Boys	10	3·10	0·74	77·5
				Girls	19	2·90	0·81	72·4
Tom Sawyer	G	12	None	Mixed	24	2·46	1·06	61·5
				Boys	17	2·65	1·12	66·2
				Girls	7	2·00	0·82	50·0
Tom Sawyer	S/M	12	2/3	Mixed	24	3·21	0·51	80·2
				Boys	11	3·27	0·47	81·8
				Girls	13	3·15	0·56	78·8

BOOK TITLE	SCHOOL	AGE	STREAM	SEX	NO. IN CLASS	MEAN	STANDARD DEVIATION	PER CENT
Tom Sawyer	G	11	1/3	Mixed	33	3·33	0·69	83·3
				Boys	14	3·14	0·66	78·6
				Girls	19	3·47	0·70	86·8
Silas Marner	G (D.G.)	13	None	Girls	26	2·27	0·96	56·7
Silas Marner	G (D.G.)	13	None	Girls	29	2·76	0·95	69·0
The Ashworth Growler	S/M	12	3/3	Mixed	18	3·11	0·83	77·8
				Boys	6	3·33	0·52	83·3
				Girls	12	3·00	0·95	75·0
The History of Mr Polly	S/M	14	2/3	Mixed	25	2·92	0·76	73·0
				Boys	12	2·92	0·90	72·9
				Girls	13	2·92	0·64	73·1
The History of Mr Polly	G (V.A.)	14	None	Boys	31	2·61	0·88	65·3
The Road to Wigan Pier	S/M	15	1/2	Mixed	24	2·25	1·07	56·3
				Boys	13	2·31	1·32	57·7
				Girls	11	2·18	0·75	54·5

Rush to Judgement	S/M	14	3/4	Mixed	26	2·62	0·70	65·4
				Boys	16	2·50	0·63	62·5
				Girls	10	2·80	0·79	70·0
Family from One End Street	S/M	11	None	Mixed	29	3·66	0·48	91·4
				Boys	16	3·50	0·52	87·5
				Girls	13	3·85	0·38	96·2
Short Stories for Girls	G (D.G.)	13	None	Girls	19	2·90	0·46	72·4
Short Stories for Girls	G (D.G.)	13	None	Girls	22	3·05	0·21	76·1
Wind in the Willows	G	11	None	Girls	28	2·93	0·86	73·2
Five Children and It	S/M	11	1/3	Girls	26	3·15	0·93	78·8
Geordie	S/M	13	1/2	Mixed	28	2·89	0·79	72·3
				Boys	14	2·71	1·07	67·9
				Girls	14	3·07	0·27	76·8
A Waltz through the Hills	S/M	14	None	Girls	21	3·10	0·44	77·4
The Pearl	S/M	13	2/4	Girls	33	2·85	0·97	71·2
Brave New World	Ind. B.P.	14/15	None	Boys	22	3·18	0·85	79·5

BOOK TITLE	SCHOOL	AGE	STREAM	SEX	NO. IN CLASS	MEAN	STANDARD DEVIATION	PER CENT
Moonfleet	Ind. B.Pr.	9/12	2/2	Boys	17	2·77	0·75	69·1
King Solomon's Mines	S/M	11	2/2	Boys	28	3·64	0·68	91·1
The Way of Danger	S/M	12	2/4	Girls	22	3·32	0·72	83·0
Bitter Herbs	S/M	14	2/3	Girls	9	2·89	0·60	72·2
Bitter Herbs	S/M	14	2/4	Girls	36	2·58	0·69	64·6
Men and Gods	G (D.G.)	11	None	Girls	29	2·90	0·82	72·4
Pilgrim's Progress	Ind.	12	3/4	Girls	23	2·74	0·69	68·5
Diary of Anne Frank	G	14	None	Girls	21	2·71	1·01	67·9
Reflections[1]	Ind. B.P.	14/15	None	Boys	23	2·39	0·84	59·8
Totals				Mixed	1117	2·88	0·87	72·0
				Boys	458	2·89	0·93	72·3
				Girls	659	2·87	0·82	71·8

[1] Although *Reflections* is not intended to be a class reader in the ordinary sense, it is certainly used as such by some teachers and thus appears in the table.

Appendix B

THE MOST POPULAR BOOKS REPORTED ON

i.e. five or more questionnaires returned

AUTHOR	TITLE	AGE-RANGE
Austen, Jane	*Pride and Prejudice*	14–15
Barnes, Douglas (Ed.)	*Short Stories of Our Time*	13–15
Brontë, Charlotte	*Jane Eyre*	12–14
Day Lewis, C.	*The Otterbury Incident*	11–13
Dickens, Charles	*David Copperfield*	11–14
Dickens, Charles	*Great Expectations*	12–15
Dickens, Charles	*Oliver Twist*	12–14
Dickens, Charles	*A Tale of Two Cities*	13–15
Durrell, Gerald	*My Family and Other Animals*	12–15
Eliot, George	*Silas Marner*	13–15
Frank, Anne	*Diary of Anne Frank*	13–15
Golding, William	*Lord of the Flies*	12–15
Grahame, Kenneth	*The Wind in the Willows*	11–12
Hardy, Thomas	*Far from the Madding Crowd*	14–15
Lee, Laurie	*Cider with Rosie*	13–15
Marshall, James Vance	*Walkabout* ('The Children')	12–13
Meade Falkner, J.	*Moonfleet*	12–13
Morrow, Honore	*The Splendid Journey*	11–13
Orwell, George	*Animal Farm*	11–15
Schaefer, J.	*Shane*	12–14
Serraillier, Ian	*The Silver Sword*	11–14
Shute, Neville	*A Town Like Alice*	14–15
Steinbeck, John	*The Pearl*	13–15
Stevenson, R. L.	*Treasure Island*	11–12
Tolkien, J. R.	*The Hobbit*	11–12
Twain, Mark	*Tom Sawyer*	11–13

AUTHOR	TITLE	AGE-RANGE
Wells, H. G.	*The History of Mr Polly*	14–15
Wyndham, John	*The Day of the Triffids*	13–15

As I have remarked elsewhere, the most notable fact about this list is its brevity. The complete list (Appendix C) shows that a large number of titles are being successfully used. However, with the exception of *Lord of the Flies*, *Animal Farm* and *The Silver Sword*, there is little marked agreement about what titles are most successful.

Appendix C

A COMPLETE LIST OF ALL BOOKS REPORTED ON

AUTHOR	TITLE	AGE-RANGE
Abrahams, Peter	*Tell Freedom*	14
Austen, Jane	*Northanger Abbey*	14
Austen, Jane	*Pride and Prejudice*	14–15
Baldwin, Michael	*Grandad with Snails*	11–13
Barnes, Douglas (ed.)	*Short Stories of Our Time*	13–15
Barnes and Egford (ed.)	*Twentieth Century Short Stories*	13–15
Barstow, Stan	*A Kind of Loving*	15
Bates, H. E.	*The Darling Buds of May*	15
Bates, H. E.	*Fair Stood the Wind for France*	15
Bawden, Nina	*On the Run*	12
Beddington, Roy	*The Pigeon and the Boy*	13
Bell, Harry (ed.)	*Thirteen Short Stories*	11
Bennett, Arnold	*The Card*	14
Berna, Paul	*A Hundred Million Francs*	11
Comp. by Black, E. L., and J. P. Parry	*Aspects of the Short Story*	15
Bradbury, Ray	*The Day it Rained for Ever*	14
Braithwaite, E. R.	*To Sir with Love*	15
Brickhill, Paul	*Reach for the Sky*	14
Brontë, Charlotte	*Jane Eyre*	12–15
Brontë, Charlotte	*Villette*	15
Brontë, Emily	*Wuthering Heights*	14–15
Broster, D. K.	*Flight of the Heron*	15
Brown, Douglas (ed.)	*A Book of Modern Prose*	15
Retold by Brown, Roy F.	*The Legend of Ulysses*	11

AUTHOR	TITLE	AGE-RANGE
Buchan, John	*The Thirty-Nine Steps*	12–13
Buck, Pearl	*O-Lan* (adapted from *The Good Earth*)	14
Bullocke, J. G. (ed.)	*The Harrap Book of Modern Short Stories*	13–14
Bunyan, John	*The Pilgrim's Progress*	11–13
Burnford, Sheila	*The Incredible Journey*	13
Burton (ed.)	*Modern Short Stories*	13–14
Carroll, Lewis	*Alice in Wonderland* and *Through the Looking-Glass*	11
Cavanagh, Nicholas	*Night Cargoes*	12–13
Church, Richard	*The Cave*	11
Churchill, Winston S.	*My Early Life*	14–15
Cleary, Beverley	*Fifteen*	14
Cleary, John	*Sundowners*	14–15
Collins, Wilkie	*The Moonstone*	14–15
Conan Doyle, A.	*The Hound of the Baskervilles*	13–14
Conan Doyle, A.	*The Lost World*	13
Conrad, Joseph	*Lord Jim*	15
Davies, W. H.	*Autobiography of a Super Tramp*	13
Day Lewis, C.	*The Otterbury Incident*	11–13
Dickens, Charles	*A Christmas Carol*	11
Dickens, Charles	*David Copperfield*	11–14
Dickens, Charles	*'David Copperfield as a Boy'*	11–12
Dickens, Charles	*Great Expectations*	12–15
Dickens, Charles	*Oliver Twist*	12–14
Dickens, Charles	*Pickwick Papers*	13
Dickens, Charles	*Tale of Two Cities*	13–15
Dixon, Stratta and Clements	*Reflections*	14
Downing, Charles	*Russian Tales and Legends*	13
du Maurier, Daphne	*Jamaica Inn*	13
du Maurier, Daphne	*Rebecca*	14
Dunford, Elaine (ed.)	*Short Stories for Girls*	13
Durrell, Gerald	*Drunken Forest*	14–15
Durrell, Gerald	*My Family and Other Animals*	12–15
Durrenmatt, Friedrich	*The Pledge*	15
Eliot, George	*The Mill on the Floss*	13
Eliot, George	*Silas Marner*	13–15
Farre, Rowena	*Seal Morning*	13–14

AUTHOR	TITLE	AGE-RANGE
Fitzpatrick, Sir James Percy	*Jock of the Bushveld*	12
Comp. by Flower, M.	*First Book of Modern Prose*	13
Forester, C. S.	*The African Queen*	13
Forester, C. S.	*Brown on Resolution*	15
Forester, C. S.	*The Gun*	13–15
Forester, C. S.	*The Happy Return*	13
Frank, Anne	*The Diary of Anne Frank*	13–15
Gallico, Paul	*Flowers for Mrs Harris*	13
Gallico, Paul	*Jennie*	12
Gallico, Paul	*The Small Miracle*	12
Garfield, Leon	*Smith*	12
Garnett, Eve	*The Family from One End Street*	11–12
Garnett, Eve	*Further Adventures of the Family from One End Street*	11
Gaskell, Mrs	*Cranford*	12
Glaskin, G. M.	*A Waltz through the Hills*	12–14
Godden, Rumer	*An Episode of Sparrows*	13
Golding, William	*Lord of the Flies*	12–15
Grahame, Kenneth	*The Wind in the Willows*	11–12
Graves, Robert	*Goodbye to All That*	15
Greene, Graham	*Brighton Rock*	14
Guillot, René (trans. Gwen Marsh)	*Kpo the Leopard*	11–12
Haggard, Rider H.	*King Solomon's Mines*	11–14
Haggard, Rider H.	*She*	14
Haig-Brown, R.	*The Whale People*	14
Hardy, Thomas	*Far from the Madding Crowd*	14–15
Hardy, Thomas	*The Mayor of Casterbridge*	14
Hardy, Thomas	*Tess of the D'Urbevilles*	15
Hardy, Thomas	*Under the Greenwood Tree*	12
Harnett, Cynthia	*The Wool Pack*	11
Hassel, Sven	*The Legion of the Damned*	14
Hemingway, Ernest	*The Old Man and the Sea*	12–14
Hodgson Burnett, F.	*The Secret Garden*	11–12
Holbrook, David (ed.)	*People and Diamonds*	14
Homer (retold by F. F. Dodd)	*Stories from Homer*	11
Homer (trans. E. V. Rieu)	*The Odyssey of Homer*	13

AUTHOR	TITLE	AGE-RANGE
Homer (trans. R. D. Wormald)	*The Odyssey of Homer*	13
Household, Geoffrey	*Rogue Male*	14
Household, Geoffrey	*The Spanish Cave*	12
Household, Geoffrey	*Watcher in the Shadows*	15
Hughes, Thomas	*Tom Brown's School Days*	11
Hughes, Richard	*High Wind in Jamaica*	13–15
Hunter, Jim (ed.)	*Modern Short Stories*	15
Huxley, Aldous	*Brave New World*	14–15
Irwin, Margaret	*Still She Wished for Company*	15
Jefferies, Richard	*After London*	13
Jepson, R. W. (ed.)	*Short Stories Old and New*	15
Jerome, Jerome K.	*Three Men in a Boat*	15
Kästner, E.	*Emil and the Detectives*	11
Kennett, John	*The Ashworth Growler*	12
Lane, Mark	*Rush to Judgement*	15
Latham, Ronald (trans.)	*The Travels of Marco Polo*	13
Laundes, J. Selby	*Canterbury Gallop*	12
Laurence, Gordon (ed.)	*Take a Look*	14
Lawrence, D. H.	*Sons and Lovers*	14–15
Lawrence, T. E.	*Seven Pillars of Wisdom (selection from)*	14
Le Carré, John	*The Spy who Came in from the Cold*	14
Lee, Harper	*To Kill a Mockingbird*	14–15
Lee, Laurie	*Cider with Rosie*	13–15
Lewis, C. S.	*The Lion, the Witch and the Wardrobe*	11
Lewis, C. S.	*Out of the Silent Planet*	14
Lewis, C. S.	*The Silver Chair*	11
London, Jack	*Call of the Wild*	12–14
London, Jack	*White Fang*	12
Macken, Walter	*God Made Sunday*	14
Maclean, Alistair	*Guns of Navarone*	15
Mankowitz, Wolf	*A Kid for Two Farthings*	12–15
Marland, Michael (ed.)	*A Sillitoe Selection*	15
Marshall, James Vance	*Walkabout ('The Children')*	12–13
Masefield, John	*Jim Davis*	11–12
Masefield, John	*Lost Endeavour*	13
Masefield, John	*Martin Hyde*	12
Masters, John	*The Deceivers*	15

AUTHOR	TITLE	AGE-RANGE
Matthewman, Phyllis	*The Mystery of Snake Island*	12
Maxwell, Gavin	*A Ring of Bright Water*	12
Meade Falkner, J.	*Moonfleet*	12–14
Melville, H.	*Moby Dick* (the whaling story from, ed. Clifton Mead)	13
Milne, A. A.	*Red House Mystery*	14
Minco, Margo	*Bitter Herbs*	14
Mitchison, Naomi	*The Land the Ravens Found*	11
Monsarrat, Nicholas	*The Cruel Sea* (school edit.)	14–15
Moody, H. L. B. (ed.)	*Facing Facts*	14
Morrow, Honore	*The Splendid Journey*	11–13
Morse, Elizabeth	*Chang*	11
Nesbit, E.	*Five Children and It*	11
Nichols, Freda	*The Milldale Riot*	13
Norton, Mary	*The Borrowers*	12
Orwell, George	*Animal Farm*	11–15
Orwell, George	*Nineteen Eighty-Four*	15
Orwell, George	*The Road to Wigan Pier*	15
Paliakov, Nicolai	*Coco the Clown*	11–12
Paton, Alan	*Cry the Beloved Country*	14–15
Priestley, J. B.	*The Good Companions*	15
Quiller-Couch, A. (ed.)	*Junior Modern Essays*	13
Rawicz, Slavomir	*The Long Walk*	13–15
Rawlings, M.	*The Yearling*	11
Reade, Miss	*Village School*	12–13
Richter, Conrad	*The Light in the Forest*	11
Rowe, A. W. (ed.)	*People Like Us*	14–15
Sassoon, Siegfried	*Memoirs of an Infantry Officer*	15
Schaefer, J.	*Shane*	12–14
Serraillier, Ian	*The Enchanted Island*	14
Serraillier, Ian	*The Silver Sword*	11–14
Serraillier, Ian	*Treasure Ahead*	11
Serraillier, Ian	*The Way of Danger*	11–13
Sewell, Anna	*Black Beauty*	11–12
Sherman, D. R.	*Old Mali and the Boy*	12–14
Shute, Neville	*The Pied Piper*	14–15
Shute, Neville	*A Town Like Alice*	14–15
Sillitoe, A.	*The Loneliness of the Long Distance Runner*	14–15
Smith, Dodie	*The Hundred and One Dalmatians*	11

AUTHOR	TITLE	AGE-RANGE
Solzhenitsyn, Alexander	*One Day in the Life of Ivan Denisovich*	14
Sperry, Armstrong	*The Boy who Was Afraid*	11–14
Steinbeck, John	*The Grapes of Wrath*	15
Steinbeck, John	*Of Mice and Men*	14–15
Steinbeck, John	*The Pearl*	13–15
Steinbeck, John	*The Red Pony*	11
Stevenson, R. L.	*The Black Arrow* (retold by John Kennett)	12
Stevenson, R. L.	*Kidnapped*	12–15
Stevenson, R. L.	*Treasure Island*	11–12
Strong, L. A. G.	*King Richard's Land*	12
Sutcliffe, Rosemary	*Eagle of the Ninth*	11
Retold by Sutcliffe, Rosemary	*Beowulf*	11
Swift, Jonathan	*Gulliver's Travels*	13–14
Synge, John M.	*The Aran Islands*	14–15
Thomas, W. B.	*Dare to Be Free*	13
Thompson, Flora	*Lark Rise to Candleford*	14–15
Thornton and Tomkins (ed.)	*Fifteen Prose Pieces*	13
Thurber, James	*The Thurber Carnival*	13
Tolkien, J. R. R.	*The Fellowship of the Ring*	12
Tolkien, J. R. R.	*The Hobbit*	11–12
Tolkien, J. R. R.	*Lord of the Rings*	11–12
Townsend, John Rowe	*Gumble's Yard*	11–13
Trease, Geoffrey	*Cue for Treason*	11–12
Treece, Henry	*Legions of the Eagle*	12
Twain, Mark	*Huckleberry Finn*	12–14
Twain, Mark	*Tom Sawyer*	11–13
Twain, Mark	*Tom Sawyer* (retold by J. Kennett)	12
Ullman, James Ramsay	*Third Man on the Mountain*	13–14
Uttley, A.	*The Country Child*	11–13
Van der Post, L.	*Lost World of the Kalahari* (abridged)	13–14
Verne, Jules	*Journey to the Centre of the Earth*	13
Walker, David	*Geordie*	13–14
Waterhouse, Keith	*Billy Liar*	14–15
Waterhouse, Keith	*There Is a Happy Land*	14

AUTHOR	TITLE	AGE-RANGE
Warner, Rex	*Greeks and Trojans*	13
Warner, Rex	*Men and Gods*	11–12
Welch, Denton	*A Voice through a Cloud*	14
Wells, H. G.	*The History of Mr Polly*	14–15
Wells, H. G.	*The Invisible Man*	13
Wells, H. G.	*Kipps*	14–15
Wells, H. G.	*Short Stories*, Volume I	14
White, T. H.	*The Sword in the Stone*	12–13
Whitehead, Frank (ed.)	*Off Beat*	13
Wibberley, Leonard	*The Mouse that Roared*	15
Wilder, Thornton	*The Bridge of San Luis Rey*	14
Wilder, Thornton	*The Ides of March*	15
Williams, Eric	*The Wooden Horse*	15
Woolf, Virginia	*Flush*	14
Wong, Jade Snow	*Fifth Chinese Daughter*	13
Wyndham, John	*The Chrysalids*	13–15
Wyndham, John	*The Day of the Triffids*	13–15

A very small number of books which were reported on have not been included in this list, because they were in fact course books and not reading books. It could be argued that *Reflections* is not a 'class reader', but I have included it as it is referred to in the text.

I did draw up a list of all the publishers of the individual titles, but it became so complex as to be probably confusing. As time went on it would have become inaccurate and positively misleading. Thus for the publishers of individual titles, teachers are referred to the current publishers' catalogues.

Appendix D

SCHOOLS VISITED IN THE COURSE OF THE PROJECT

I am particularly grateful for a great deal of assistance from the Heads and from the English Departments of the following schools which were visited in the course of the Project.

Aldersbrook Secondary School	London
Ashford School	Ashford
Baas Hill School	Broxbourne
Bishop Vesey's Grammar School	Sutton Coldfield
Bradford Girls' Grammar School	Bradford
Brook Comprehensive School	Sheffield
Collenswood Secondary School	Stevenage
Corner Hall Girls' Secondary School	Hemel Hempstead
Cranleigh Preparatory School	Cranleigh
Crown Woods Comprehensive School	London
Emanuel School	London
Fairfax High School	Sutton Coldfield
Forest Fields Grammar School	Nottingham
London Colney County Secondary School	London Colney
Marlborough College	Marlborough
Newland High School	Hull
Pear Tree Boys' School	Derby
Riland Bedford High School	Sutton Coldfield
Royal Grammar School	Lancaster
Shelton Lock County Secondary School	Derby
Simon Langton's Girls' School	Canterbury
Sir Joseph Williamson's Mathematical School	Rochester
Stanmer County Secondary School	Brighton
Stocksbridge Secondary School	Stocksbridge
Sutton-in-Ashfield Girls' Grammar School	Sutton-in-Ashfield
Trescobeas County Secondary School	Falmouth
Victoria County School for Girls	Watford
Walthamstow Hall	Sevenoaks

Appendix E

AN ACKNOWLEDGEMENT

Many teachers I met and who wrote to me may recognize themselves somewhere in the pages of this report. The anonymity which such a report demands means that their substantial contributions become obscured and remain unrecognized and unacknowledged. I would thus particularly like to salute and make public acknowledgement to the following teachers whose work has been extensively drawn upon, described or discussed in great detail, very often in their own words.

S. L. Clark
Ian Davie
Marilyn Davies
N. J. Ellis
G. P. Fox
Elizabeth Grugeon
Brian Hague
Josephine Hall
John Jenkins
Ruth Read
Eileen Thompson
N. M. Thomson
G. G. Watkins
S. C. Watson
M. G. Wynne